Getting and Keeping the Job

Getting and Keeping the Job

Success in Business and Technical Careers

VAL CLARK
Spokane Community College

Allyn and Bacon
Boston • London • Toronto • Sydney • Tokyo • Singapore

Series editor: Virginia Lanigan
Series editorial assistant: Bridget Keane
Manufacturing buyer: Suzanne Lareau

Copyright © 1999 by Allyn & Bacon
A Viacom Company
Needham Heights, MA 02494

Internet: www.abacon.com

Library of Congress Cataloging-in-Publication Data

Clark, Val.
    Getting and keeping the job : success in business and technical
careers / Val Clark.
        p.   cm.
    Includes index.
    ISBN 0-205-28920-7
    1. Job hunting.   2. Business—Vocational guidance.   3. Industrial
technicians—Vocational guidance.   I. Title.
    HF5382.7.C55   1999   98-30268
    650.14—dc21   CIP

Printed in the United States of America
10 9 8 7 6 5 4 3 2 1   02 01 00 99 98

To Lois J. Roach, my mentor, inspiration, and friend.
Lois is the person who originated many of the concepts
in this textbook.

Contents

CHAPTER THREE   **Creating Interest in Yourself   76**
Learning Objectives   76

Part II

CHAPTER FOUR   **What Was That You Said? Telephoning and Listening   104**
Learning Objectives   104

Preface

What communication tools do employers expect job applicants to use *during* employment interviews for technical and business positions, and which communication tools do employees need to be successful *on* the job after being hired? Prior to writing this text, surveys were conducted asking employers these questions. The first survey was completed in 1983 and was repeated in 1992 and 1998 to determine employers' answers to these important questions.

Additional employers have been consulted to provide you, the job applicant, as well as you, the instructor, with an accurate picture of which communication skills employers anticipate needing from the members of the work force as we move toward the year 2000. All of this data is integrated within the text, along with a copy of the survey.

Based on this research and several years of teaching Job Communication Skills and Speech for Business Courses for business and technical students from various career fields, the ideas for this book were developed and are presented here to help applicants be thoroughly prepared *for* job interviews and to help them to be able to communicate effectively *during* the interview. Guidelines are also presented for equipping new employees with communication tools necessary for relating to customers and co-workers more productively *on* the job after they are hired. A brief overview of the text is included in this preface.

OVERVIEW

The book is divided into three parts. Each chapter in the three sections has suggestions for building employment networks and adjusting to cultural differences. These suggestions are embedded in the chapters along with practical work examples and skill exercises, titled "Tools of Communication." In addition, there are case studies, a "Stress Less" exercise, a major project, and discussion questions at the end of each chapter. All of these are developed to reinforce the learning objectives of the chapter.

Part I   *Chapters 1–3 focus* on being prepared for the job search through the analysis of attitudes, skills, communication styles, and previous work experience. Resume and portfolio preparation ideas are presented, accompanied by techniques for researching companies, writing cover letters, and completing accurate application forms.

Part II   *Chapters 4 and 5 discuss* the importance of listening proficiency, include different types of employment interviews and present interviewing questions with appropriate and inappropriate responses.

Part III *Chapters 6 and 7 stress* the need for effective relationships with customers and co-workers through understanding perceptual and cultural differences. This section also presents the ideas for working productively in teams by utilizing problem-solving skills. Eighty-eight percent of 180 employers surveyed in 1992 indicated that employees need problem-solving skills. Additional employers consulted in 1995 and 1996 emphasized the need for self-managed work teams and provided further confirmation of the need for problem-solving skills and the use of the critical thinking process.

A NOTE TO INSTRUCTORS

This material is designed to provide you with exercises, evaluation criteria, and feedback forms, along with practical examples for technical and business students to add *communication* tools to those already acquired.

Using the various Tools of Communication exercises as in-class or out-of-class assignments can reinforce the acquisition of students' communication skills while reducing your class preparation time.

A NOTE TO STUDENTS

If you read the text carefully, complete the Tools of Communication exercises thoughtfully, and practice using these Tools regularly, you can be better prepared when applying *for* a job and be better equipped for succeeding *on* the job. In addition, try the Stress Less exercises toward the end of each chapter for reducing the frustrations of the job search and while working on the job.

ACKNOWLEDGMENTS

Great appreciation is extended to the following reviewers who offered many excellent and helpful suggestions: Jeffrey W. Belding, DeVry Institute; Wendolyn E. Tetlow, DeVry Institute; and Susan H. Chin, DeVry Institute.

Also, this effort could not have been produced without the assistance and outstanding computer skills of Lorie Lee and, later, Janet Jay.

In addition, I am most grateful to the many employers who responded to the surveys providing specific information about the communication skills employees need.

Nancy Forsyth, Virginia Lanigan, Jenine Duffey, and Bridget Keene at Allyn and Bacon have been so helpful in providing advice and encouragement during the publishing process.

Especially, I want to thank my husband, Dean, who has been incredibly supportive.

Introduction: About You and Your Search for the Right Employment Position

Now you have completed most of your training and are ready to look for employment. Before knocking on employers' doors, it is usually necessary to do some additional preparation.

- **Be prepared** by analyzing your personal strengths, attitudes, assets, and areas for growth.
- **Be prepared** by organizing a written sales campaign about yourself before you look for employment
- **Be prepared** by researching companies you are interested in working for to be better equipped to ask and answer questions about these companies.
- **Be prepared** by knowing which communication skills employers expect during the job interview and on the job.
- **Be prepared** by understanding customers' needs.
- **Be prepared** by knowing how to work as a team member. Many companies, large and small, desire employees with teamwork skills.

This book is full of suggestions, ideas, and information about some of the best ways of analyzing yourself and your abilities, along with resume samples and portfolio suggestions to help you present yourself effectively. Also included are sample letters of application, methods for researching companies you want to work for, and recommendations that describe successful ways of communicating during the job interview with confidence and professionalism.

Getting the job is only the first step up the stairway to job success. **Succeeding on the job** will be the next step to advance in your career of choice, so suggestions for communicating effectively with customers and co-workers are also included in the text. On-the-job communication competency can be acquired through learning how to apply specific communication skills such as paraphrasing, perception checking, building positive communication climates, using creative problem-solving techniques, and applying the critical thinking process while working alone or as a team member.

CHAPTER ONE

Analyzing Yourself and the Trends of the Job Market

LEARNING OBJECTIVES

1. Understand the value of a positive attitude, and evaluate your own attitude.

2. Learn techniques for improving a neutral or negative attitude.

3. Assess your transferable job skills and analyze your previous employment experiences.

4. Learn how to analyze and use different communication styles

5. Know the communication skills employers expect during job interviews.

6. Examine recent trends in the workplace.

7. Learn how to evaluate your abilities according to the changing workplace.

8. Research employers to determine the communication skills they want to hear applicants discuss during interviews.

Whether you will be looking for your first job, returning to the job market after a long absence, or just searching for a more challenging position, there is a key to your success—and that key is a positive attitude.

1.1 TYPES OF ATTITUDES

Attitudes are usually referred to as:

1. **Positive:**

Curious,

determined,

enthusiastic,

honest,

optimistic.

2. **Neutral:** Uncaring, apathetic, "I'll just do my time"

3. **Negative:** Defensive, fearful of others' opinions
of the unknown
of being wrong

1.2 DEVELOPING A POSITIVE ATTITUDE

Believe in your training. Believe in your knowledge, in your skills, and in your ability to communicate with others. **Believe in yourself!** Above all, do not sell yourself short.

Why is a positive attitude important? Most employers believe a negative attitude costs them money in terms of lost production and lower employee morale.

WORLD OF WORK A supervisor at a manufacturing plant said, "One negative person can infect fifteen other workers." He went on to say that after two negative workers were dismissed, following verbal and written warnings about their negative attitudes, production increased and the remaining employees' attitudes improved greatly.

Because a positive attitude is such a critical factor contributing to job success, a good place to start is by asking yourself some general questions about your attitude. Is it positive? Negative? Neutral? To determine this, complete the Tools of Communication exercise by doing the following:

Part A   Mark your responses to six statements.

Part B   Give this segment to someone who knows you well, is in your program, or works with you. Ask that person to mark how *he or she* perceives your attitude.

Part C   Compare your analysis of your attitude with the other person's perception of your attitude. Are there differences or areas where you might improve your attitude?

Evaluating Your Attitude, Part A

Instructions
Put an X on the number you think best describes you. Now go back and connect the X's with a continuous line. The higher numbers toward the right indicate a more positive attitude. Is your attitude positive? Negative? Neutral? (Circle one of these three options after connecting the X's.)

1	2	3	4
I dislike changes in routine procedures and organized structure.			I enjoy frequent changes in what I do.

1	2	3	4
I have difficulty working with people of diverse background and beliefs.			I like working with people of diverse backgrounds and beliefs.

1	2	3	4
It is difficult to listen to people who disagree with me.			I listen carefully when someone expresses an idea or opinion that differs from mine.

1	2	3	4
When someone points out my mistakes, I tend to close up or yell at them.			When someone points out my mistakes, I usually am able to listen and evaluate what they say objectively.

1	2	3	4
When I meet new people, it's hard to know what to say.			When I meet new people, I am comfortable talking to them.

1	2	3	4
It's difficult for me to communicate with those in authority (employers, instructors).			I enjoy communicating with those in authority.

Evaluating Your Attitude, Part B

Instructions
Please rate how you perceive my attitude. Be honest, so that I can learn about myself from your assessment. Thank you in advance for your thoughtful evaluations and answers.

Put an X on the number that you think best describes me: _____ (your name) _____
Then go back and connect your X's with a continuous line. How do you perceive my attitude. Positive? Negative? Neutral? (Circle one.) Higher numbers reflect a more positive attitude.

1	2	3	4
Dislikes changes in routine procedures and organized structure.			Enjoys frequent changes and working out details along the way.
1	2	3	4
Is uncomfortable working with people of diverse backgrounds and beliefs.			Prefers working with people of diverse backgrounds and beliefs.
1	2	3	4
Has difficulty listening to people with differing opinions.			Listens carefully when someone expresses an idea or opinion that differs.
1	2	3	4
Gets upset and either closes up or yells when someone points out his/her mistakes.			Usually listens and evaluates carefully when mistakes are pointed out.
1	2	3	4
Is uncomfortable and quiet when meeting new people.			Is comfortable when talking to new people.
1	2	3	4
Has difficulty communicating with those in authority (instructors, employers).			Communicates easily with those in authority.

In the space below, please write a short response about your analysis of my attitude.

What are my communication strengths in this career field? Please suggest some areas for growth in communication:

_____

_____

Signed by evaluator,

_____

Evaluating Your Attitude, Part C

Instructions
After completing your personal attitude survey, compare it with the one you received from the other person. Where do they agree? Disagree? What is your attitude? What are your strengths? What would you most like to change, if anything? Why? What are your communication strengths and areas for growth?

_____

_____

_____

_____

_____

_____

_____

_____

_____

_____

_____

Often you can change a situation by modifying your attitude toward it, even if you cannot alter what has happened. Maybe you have made some bad choices or some mistakes, but learning from mistakes means you have not lost knowledge because of those negative experiences. The only way to grow and learn is to have the attitude, "I want to take risks and learn from my mistakes." Tom Jeske, a carpentry instructor, emphasized this point when he told a student who was repairing a project, "A mistake is only a mistake if you don't fix it."

Remember:

Be INQUISITIVE

NOT INFERIOR or INDIFFERENT!!

Your attitude is the food you choose to serve your mind!

If you find your "attitude food" is not very flavorful, you can do something to improve the taste. What can you do? Try some of the ideas in the next section.

If you are in the neutral or negative zone, try the following idea to develop the more positive attitude that is so necessary for success both during an employment interview and later on for success in your career.

Even if you have a generally positive attitude, it will be very helpful to keep an attitude log throughout your life and review it when you encounter a "down" time. Dan Miller, a motivational speaker, encourages us to be "dream makers, not dreambreakers." This can happen only when we are willing to persist in our efforts to reach our goals by maintaining a positive attitude.

Can a positive attitude really pay off?

WORLD OF WORK   Gil Leon, vice-president of Motor Works, an engine remanufacturing company, hires many employees with no mechanical experience. All that is required, Leon points out, is "Attitude, attendance, and the ability to learn."

Incidentally, this company shared 30 percent of its 1996 profits with its 80 employees, 12 days before Christmas. The employees' bonus checks, which varied according to length of employment with the company, ranged from $180 for those with three weeks of work to $8,000 for those with a three-year employment history at Motor Works. The *total* sum of the profits the company shared with its employees was $428,000! (Boggs, A1)

TOOLS OF COMMUNICATION

Attitude Log

Instructions
At least three times a week for the next three weeks, write down something positive that happened to you or to someone around you. This could be something as simple as a good meal or as complex as developing a new design.

Week 1: **1.** _____

2. _____

3. _____

Week 2: **1.** _____

2. _____

3. _____

Week 3: **1.** _____

2. _____

3. _____

TOOLS OF COMMUNICATION

Instructions

Working in pairs or teams, think of negative comments you have heard or experienced that contributed to a negative work environment. Then decide how these situations should have been managed to produce a positive workplace. Share your results with the class.

If you are working alone, interview two employers who hire people in your career area. Ask them how they handle employees who contribute to a negative atmosphere. The results of these interviews can also be shared in class.

There are a number of additional things you can do to maintain a positive outlook during the competition of the job search:

- One way to improve your attitude is to read. Your mind acts on what you feed it, so read motivational materials or stories about those who have made building blocks out of roadblocks. Then analyze what you have read. Ask yourself, "Why and how did this person succeed? How can I apply this author's ideas to my life?"
- Cultivating friendships with people who maintain a positive view of life will also be helpful. Negative relationships can affect a person very quickly. While you are looking for employment, you do not need to hear discouraging words.

WORLD OF WORK

Employers from technical fields such as a fluid power company in Seattle, Washington, and Bonneville Power in Spokane, Washington, emphasize the fact that they do not even want to *interview* prospective employees who have negative attitudes or are untrained in the area of communication.

Once you have analyzed your attitude, it will be useful to assess your personal job skills and determine where and how you developed those skills. This assessment is important because employers need to know which skills you will contribute to their company. These skills, often referred to as **transferable skills,** are specific skills useful in any career. You will need to be able to discuss them confidently with potential employers.

TOOLS OF COMMUNICATION

Transferable Skills Assessment

Instructions

Using the list provided, consider the skills you possess. Put an X by those you think you already have. When you have done that, go back over the list and make a note of how or where you developed each skill.

This list is by no means exhaustive. Add more skills as you think of them. You will want to incorporate these descriptive words along with *where* you acquired them in your resume and cover letters. Also be prepared to discuss them during job interviews.

_____	Analyzing _____	_____	Functioning _____
_____	Beginning _____	_____	Leading _____
_____	Calculating _____	_____	Listening _____
_____	Comparing _____	_____	Managing _____
_____	Computing _____	_____	Observing _____
_____	Constructing _____	_____	Operating _____
_____	Contributing _____	_____	Organizing _____
_____	Conveying _____	_____	(Other) _____
_____	Counseling _____	_____	Participating _____
_____	Creating _____	_____	Performing _____
_____	Demonstrating _____	_____	Problem solving _____
_____	Designing _____	_____	Researching _____
_____	Determining _____	_____	Selling _____
_____	Developing _____	_____	Supporting _____
_____	Diagnosing _____	_____	Teaching _____
_____	Editing _____	_____	Understanding _____
_____	Evaluating _____	_____	Writing _____
_____	Examining _____		

Now it is time to examine your *specific* job experiences. Within every job, there may be activities you like and others that you dislike. Suppose you like writing reports but hate filing, or enjoy calling people to make appointments but dislike answering the phone when others go to lunch. Obviously, then, the skills you will transfer to a new job are writing and spending time talking to people, but you will want to avoid a position with low-thought repetitive filing and interruptions. "Job Analysis," Part A gives you the opportunity to review two previous jobs you have had.

Now look at this review of the past from a different perspective. Part B of the job analysis asks you to determine those values that would be important to you when evaluating any new position.

When carefully thought out, the following "Job Analysis" exercises, Parts A and B, can help you identify some of your specific employment needs and preferences. Please answer these questions carefully. The answers may help you to realize *what you need in an employment situation,* as well as *what you have to offer to an employer.*

TOOLS OF COMMUNICATION

Job Analysis, Part A

Instructions

What kinds of employment have you had in the past? List *two* jobs you have held, either part-time or full-time. What did you like and dislike about these jobs? (Use words and phrases).

Job #1–Describe	Things You Liked	Things You Disliked
Job #2–Describe	Things You Liked	Things You Disliked

Did you supervise anyone else? If so, what did you enjoy about supervision? Or do you prefer a job that does not require you to supervise others?

_____

_____

_____

Job Analysis, Part B

1. *At the present time,* is there a specific type of employment that interests you? If so, what is it? Maybe sales or service for a specific company?

_____

_____

_____

2. Would you prefer a *people-oriented job*? Or would you prefer working *more on your own* with equipment? Or would you like a *combination* of these? Explain.

_____

_____

_____

_____

3. Do you need *lots of variety and movement* during a working day, or would you *feel more comfortable behind a desk or working at a machine* most of the time? Explain.

_____

_____

_____

4. Do you picture yourself in an *indoor* or *outdoor working environment*? Explain.

_____

_____

_____

5. What needs do you have in a *working environment*? Explain. For example, are you most happy when it is reasonably quiet, clean, and uncluttered?

_____

_____

_____

6. Consider yourself as a *potential employee.* Analyze the following:

Employment Strengths	Skills You Want to Develop or Improve

7. (Optional) *Assess your monthly expenses.* Include rent or mortgage, food, utilities, gas, auto expenses, insurance, plus any other *fixed* monthly expenses. *How much monthly income* (approximate figure) do you need to meet your present life-style needs? Are you providing a second income or the only family income? If you know the kind of employment you are interested in, does the beginning pay scale meet your needs?

When you have completed the forms in these sections, summarize your ideas, skills, and abilities in a thoughtful paragraph.

Next, ask yourself which of the following values are most important when seeking employment? Circle the three most critical values in a job. In another paragraph state why they are the most significant to you.

For me it is vital that my job has:

1. Good pay
2. Creativity
3. Security—this company is going to be in business long term
4. Medical benefits
5. A good retirement plan
6. Little supervision
7. Structured supervision
8. Honesty
9. Integrity—a company known for keeping its word
10. Recognition for work well done
11. Regular work evaluations from supervisors
12. Company exhibits loyalty to customers and co-workers
13. Opportunity for advancement
14. Other values not listed above

The reason for this values assessment is to have an accurate understanding of what is important to you in terms of your needs. If your needs cannot be met by this employer, it will be difficult for *you* to maintain a productive attitude.

Now you are ready to investigate your preferred style of communication.

It's helpful to analyze communication styles to see how you compare with others in the class, in the office, or on your work team. When you understand differences in communication styles, you can learn how to adjust your communication style in order to interact with others more effectively. Because there are efficient and inefficient applications of communication styles, it will be very helpful to recognize, accommodate these styles, and motivate others according to their individual strengths and needs.

TOOLS OF COMMUNICATION

Analysis of Communication Styles

To begin to understand your favorite style of communication, finish this communication analysis.

The statement that best describes you rate . . . 7.

The next best description . . . 5.

The third analysis is given . . . 4.

The statement that least describes you . . . 2.

1. Others are likely to see me as:

useful and action-oriented. a _____

sentimental and interesting. b _____

reasonable and thoughtful. c _____

rational and a deep thinker. d _____

2. When dealing with others who have an opposing opinion, I can often get to a decision by:

finding one or two ideas to combine with others' ideas to solve problems. a _____

understanding others emotionally. b _____

remaining relaxed while helping others to see things reasonably. c _____

trusting my own skills to put ideas together. d _____

3. I am happy when I:

am able to complete more work than what was planned for the day. a _____

understand the emotions of others and help them. b _____

explain issues systematically. c _____

try new ideas that can be connected to other concepts. d _____

4. When I work on plans, I usually:

want to be certain the plans have results that are realistic to prove that my time and energy will be well spent.   a _____

want to be involved in exciting, energetic conversations with others.   b _____

focus my energy on seeing that ideas are developed in an organized manner.   c _____

want my ideas to bring something original to the project.   d _____

5. When thinking about the use of time, I think most about:

my first reactions to the situation to determine if they will mean anything later.   a _____

if what I am doing will be a significant memory.   b _____

being positive that any decisions I make are part of an organized advancement of projects.   c _____

meaningful long-term goals that will fit with my personal goals.   d _____

6. It is easy to persuade others when I am:

practical and do not talk too much.   a _____

understand others' feelings as well as my own.   b _____

reasonable and tolerant.   c _____

rationally aware of others and able to consider many different opinions.   d _____

When you finish this analysis, add the figures in each of the categories (a, b, c, d) and place that number below:

Sum of a's _____   Sum of c's _____

Sum of b's _____   Sum of d's _____

Your highest score will show your most used style for communicating with others, and your second highest score points out your secondary style. The "a" score implies a *practical* style, the "b" score an *emotional* style, the "c" score an *analytical* style, and the "d" score a *creative* style.

The following information explains efficient and inefficient uses of each of these styles of communication. These explanations can also assist in creating a more productive work environment, because you will be able to utilize each co-worker's strengths and recognize communication skills that need to be "sharpened."

Characteristics Associated with the Styles

A. Practical Style	Efficient Application	Inefficient Application
	Useful	Don't see long range
	Assertive, directional	Want attention
	Results-oriented	Self-involved
	Objective	Act first then think
	Opinion is based on what is actually seen	Lack trust in others
	Competitive	Domineering
	Confident	

A person with this style of communication could:
  Fear–being taken advantage of.
A person with this communication style probably could be:
  Motivated by–directness and confrontation.
If this is your communication style you will usually be:
  More effective–if you learn to get others' opinions, then move forward.

B. Emotional Style	Efficient Application	Inefficient Application
	Spontaneous	Impulsive
	Persuasive	Tries to manipulate others
	Empathetic	Overpersonalizes, takes things too personally
	Understands traditional values	
	Probing	Sentimental
	Analyzes self	Postponing
	Draws out feelings of others	Guilt-ridden
	Loyal	Stirs up conflict
		Subjective

A person with this style of communication could:
  Fear–loss of security due to changes in procedure or policies and/or hurting others.
A person with this communication style probably could be:
  Motivated by–the use of traditional procedures.
If this is your communication style you usually will be:
  More effective–if you do not take yourself too seriously and realize you cannot please everyone.

C. Analytical Style	Efficient Application	Inefficient Application
	Effective communicator	Talk too much
	Take time making decisions	Indecisive
	Careful	Overly cautious
	Weigh alternatives	Overly analytical
	Stabilizing	Unemotional
	Objective	Not energetic
	Rational	Controlled and controlling
	Analytical	Too serious, rigid

A person with this style of communication could:
   Fear—criticism of work, loss of harmony.
A person with this communication style probably could be:
   Motivated by—right way to proceed.
If this is your communication style, you will usually be:
   More effective—if you take risks. Be flexible, willing to move without knowing all the details.

D. Creative Style	Efficient Application	Inefficient Application
	Original	Unrealistic
	Imaginative	"Far-out"
	Creative	Fantasy-bound
	Broad-gauged, thinks about big picture	Scattered
	Charming	Sneaky
	Thinks about future	Out of touch
	Likes to think about theoretical issues	Insistent on own way
	Sticks to theories	Impractical

A person with this style of communication could:
   Fear—loss of approval.
A person with this communication style probably could be:
   Motivated by—recognition and praise in front of peers.
If this is your communication style, you will usually be:
   More effective—if you listen more and organize yourself.

How do you make use of this information? Here is a situation that explains how this analysis can be put into practical use.

WORLD OF WORK   Charlie, the manager, completes the communication styles analysis. His Practical communicator score is within two points of the very different Emotional style of communication. In other words, he recognizes the work that needs to be accomplished and yet is aware of the problems another person is having at home that are causing him to be absent, thus delaying work. This situation will probably cause Charlie some inner stress, because he clearly understands the demands of the job as well as the needs of the employee. Recognizing the source of the stress can help Charlie make more realistic decisions through "getting others' opinions before decision-making time" and "realizing that a manager can't please everyone" (p. 16).

TOOLS OF   *Instructions*
COMMUNICATION   Work with a partner, and decide how each person in the following situation could be more effective in the application of his or her communication style. Then compare your solutions with those of the rest of the class.

1. Jane, the Analytical team leader, has to complete a research assignment with her partner, Jack, who is very Practical in his style of communication. Jack just wants to finish the work and go home. If you were the leader in this situation, how would you motivate Jack?
2. Ken is the leader and probably the most creative person on the design team. He insists on presenting his ideas to the supervisor even though three members of the group do not think his ideas are practical. How could these three approach Ken to motivate him to be more practical? Should they talk to the supervisor about their ideas if Ken ignores them? How could that be accomplished in a positive way?

Next, it will be helpful to study the communication skills employers expect applicants to demonstrate during job interviews.

Workplace communication skills valued by employers on the job will be presented in Chapters Six and Seven.

1.7 WHAT DO EMPLOYERS EXPECT?

**About now, you may be asking yourself,
"Why bother with all this self-analysis?"**

When interviewing prospective employees, **34 percent** of the **200** employers in a 1998 survey* reported that the communication skill most affecting the outcome of the interview was that applicants had the ability to describe their background and qualifications clearly.

Consequently, the self-analysis steps in this chapter are essential in order to communicate abilities, assets, and attitudes effectively.

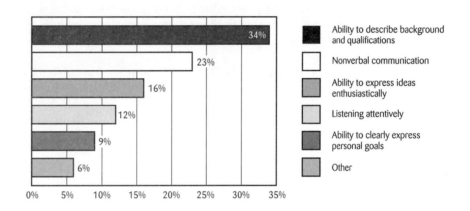

In the current job market, however, there are many other significant changes taking place. These have to do with the changing nature of work.

WORLD OF WORK   Douglas Jardine, retired president of Capilano College in Vancouver, British Columbia, observed: "Somewhere, not that long ago, I read something to the effect that a competitive world has two possibilities: You can lose. Or, if you want to win, you can change."

"A very recent echo of this assertion was made by George Hancock, president of a Canadian textile firm, when he said, 'I don't suppose that there's a company . . . that hasn't changed in some fundamental way, whether it's what they produce or how they produce it. Everybody that failed to change ain't here anymore.' "

(Leadership Connections, 1)

1. **The nature of work is changing.** Increasingly, workers need more knowledge skills than manual skills. Products are robo-factured rather than manufactured, and workers must be able to plan the work of the robot rather than simply manipulating a tool. The changing nature of work thus demands changes in the nature of education.
2. **"Work" is replacing "jobs"** as the pattern of full-time, full-year jobs gives way to work on a part-time basis, and often to work as self-employment rather than as an employee. The educational response here must recognize that entrepreneurial skills are a condition of success for the self-employed and are a great advantage to those who work for an employer.

(Leadership Connections, 3)

---

*A copy of the survey is included at the end of this chapter. A specific detailed analysis of the survey is available from the author, whose address is listed in the preface.

It is helpful to evaluate additional areas of your skills in order to market yourself more aggressively in the new "workplace without jobs." This term, "workplace without jobs," is used by Dr. William Bridges in his challenging book, *Jobshift*, to describe this phenomenon occurring in the job market in many parts of this country. His book discusses the tendency of employers to hire temporary and/or task-related workers instead of traditional full-time employees.

1.8 D.A.T.A. ANALYSIS: DESIRES, ABILITIES, TEMPERAMENT, ASSETS

In addition to analyzing your personal attitude, evaluating your previous job skills, and analyzing your communication styles, there are other changing areas to explore. To deal with these changes, Bridges suggests you answer these D.A.T.A. questions:

1. What are my **Desires?** (Not wishes such as, "I wish I would win the lottery," but desires). Supply your own desires if the following don't apply to you.
   a. I want to spend more time with my family.
   b. I want to live where it never snows.
   c. I want to be debt-free in ten years.
2. What are my unique **Abilities?** What am I good at? (Again, continue personalizing your responses to numbers 2 through 4.)
   a. Talking/relating to others.
   b. Completing a task.
   c. Finding creative solutions to problems.
3. When am I most productive and content? What's my **Temperament?**
   a. The Meyers-Briggs test is useful here. If you have access to it, look at the results as areas for growth as well as strengths.
   b. Or ask yourself questions such as, "Do I like to work alone, with others, or with an authority figure?"
4. What have I done in the past that sets me apart from someone else? What are my **Assets?**
   a. Yes, money is an asset but, more important, what is your education?
   b. Do you speak another language?
   c. Do you have experience working with people of diverse cultures?*

Additional self-analysis is useful when developing a personal portfolio (more about this in a later chapter), a resume, and when writing cover letters, whether you are applying for the more traditional business/technical position or for the temporary situations reported by Bridges in his book.

---

*W. Bridges, *Jobshift*, 77, © by William Bridges and Associates, Inc. Reprinted by permission of Addison-Wesley Longman Inc.

Your D.A.T.A.*

Instructions
Develop **your** own D.A.T.A. following the examples and ideas on the previous page:

1. What are *my* **Desires** (not wishes such as, "I wish I didn't have to work")?

_____

_____

_____

2. What are *my* unique **Abilities?** What am I good at?

_____

_____

_____

3. When am *I* most productive and content? What's my **Temperament?**

_____

_____

_____

4. What have I done in the past that sets me apart from someone else? What are my **Assets?**

_____

_____

_____

_____

*W. Bridges, *Jobshift*, 77, © by William Bridges and Associates, Inc. Reprinted by permission of Addison-Wesley Longman Inc.

All of this self-analysis may produce some stress in your life, so stop and try the following idea to reduce your stress level. You may be feeling like a wire that's overstretched and past its limits. Perhaps you may related to this frayed wire icon. Look for "Stress Less" suggestions in each of the following chapters.

STRESS LESS

Record ten little things you enjoy, such as:

Seeing a beautiful sunset

Watching a football game on TV with friends

Sanding a board to a smooth finish

Your list:

1.

2.

3.

4.

5.

6.

7.

8.

9.

10.

Often, you can reduce your stress level by pausing to remember the things you enjoy doing. Stress workshop consultant Pat Schwab says, "If you don't pause, nothing worthwhile in life will catch up with you."

CASE STUDY *A young new employee, Jane, has been exceeding all expectations and seems to be destined for an early promotion. She has a positive attitude toward work and tells others, "I am working for the Johnson Company, not for $10.50 per hour."*

Now Jane comes to you and says she is going to quit. When asked why, she says it is because the older employees are so negative that coming to work every day has become increasingly depressing. She wants to find someplace to work where other employees have a more positive attitude. If you were her supervisor, what would you do?

CHAPTER PROJECT   Call two employers in your career field, and ask them if they would be willing to complete a communication skills survey as part of a class project. If they agree, copy the following survey, and either mail the surveys or deliver them personally to the employers. Please ask the employers to sign the survey, and include the name and address of their company for verification of the assignment. Provide self-addressed, stamped envelopes for the employers to use to return the survey to you. When the surveys come back, tabulate the results and share the outcome with your class. Finally, have someone tabulate the results for the entire class, and discuss the conclusions of this research.

There is an additional advantage in conducting these surveys to complete the chapter project. The surveys can serve as a beginning for you to develop a personal network with employers in your field. The information gained can also be a useful point of reference in cover letters and/or telephone calls later, when you are seeking employment.

Building a broad-based network of employers is very beneficial for those who are job hunting. You, too, will find such a network helpful during the job-seeking process. Start constructing your network by keeping a record of your initial contacts and their responses to the surveys. Any other employers you meet or hear speak at an employment fair should be added to your list, thus widening your network of potential employers.

DISCUSSION QUESTIONS

1. Do you think a positive attitude is important in the workplace? Why or why not?
2. Which three transferable skills do you think are the most valuable?
3. Do you agree with the analysis of your communication style? Why or why not?
4. If you were an employer, which two communication skills on page 25 of the employers' survey do you think are the most important? Why?

SUMMARY

In this chapter you had the opportunity to begin your job search by analyzing:

- your attitude and learning how to improve and/or maintain it.
- your transferable job skills, previous employment, and communication styles.
- the communication skills employers expect during job interviews.
- recent trends in the changing workplace.
- how to begin to build an employment network.

COMMUNICATION SKILLS SURVEY

PLEASE HELP US BE OF GREATER SERVICE TO YOU.

In an effort to train students more effectively in the area of verbal communication skills, and to better meet your needs as an employer, we would appreciate your assistance. Will you please take a few minutes to answer this brief survey?

MARKING INSTRUCTIONS:
For each question, you are asked to circle the number or letter that most clearly indicates your thinking as to the communications skills needed in your business or industry.

1. When interviewing prospective employees, the communication skills that most affect the outcome of the interview are:

(CIRCLE TWO)

a. Ability to describe their background and qualifications

b. Ability to clearly express personal goals

c. Ability to express ideas enthusiastically

d. Listening attentively

e. Nonverbal communication (such as handshake, eye contact, or general appearance)

f. Other

(CIRCLE ONE)

2. In my opinion, the applicants I have interviewed have been able to describe their technical skills needed in a clear manner.

1	2	3	4
almost never	seldom	often	frequently

3. In my opinion, the applicants I have interviewed have had a good opinion of themselves as individuals.

1	2	3	4
almost never	seldom	often	frequently

4. My decision to hire someone has been affected by his or her ability to communicate well during the interview.

1	2	3	4
almost never	seldom	often	frequently

5. Most of my employees are able to express their opinions effectively when in a small group (3 to 10 people).

1	2	3	4
almost never	seldom	often	frequently

6. It is important that my employees are able to express their opinions in a small group.

1	2	3	4
almost never	seldom	often	frequently

7. Most of my employees are able to organize and present a short 5- to 10-minute speech to a group of 20 to 50 people.

1	2	3	4
almost never	seldom	often	frequently

8. It is important for my employees to be able to organize and present a short 5- to 10-minute speech to a group of people.

1	2	3	4
almost never	seldom	often	frequently

9. The communication skills I desire most in my employees are:

(CIRCLE TWO)

a. Listening to and following directions

b. Getting along with other employees

c. Communication with customers

d. Ability to accept criticism

e. Communication in a small group

f. Other _____

10. Please rank the three most important communication skills as they would affect the success of an employee. Rate the most important skill as number 1.

_____ Listening

_____ Prepared speaking

_____ Thinking and speaking on your feet

_____ Small-group communication

_____ Customer-related communication

_____ Employee-to-employee communication

_____ Employer-to-employee communication

_____ Problem solving

_____ Other _____

(CIRCLE ONE)

11. An employee could be dismissed because she or he did not follow verbal directions.

1	2	3	4
almost never	seldom	often	frequently

12. An employee could be dismissed because she or he did not listen to and/or relate well with the customers.

1	2	3	4
almost never	seldom	often	frequently

13. An employee could be dismissed because she or he did not get along well with other employees.

1	2	3	4
almost never	seldom	often	frequently

14. The number of people employed by this business/industry is:

1	2	3	4
0–10	11–20	21–50	over 100

Employer's name _____

Position _____

Name of Company _____

Address _____

_____

_____

CHAPTER TWO

Preparing a Report on Yourself: Resumes and Portfolios

LEARNING OBJECTIVES

1. Understand why a well-organized, error-free resume is an important part of the job search process.

2. Learn how to organize information for a resume, as well as guidelines to consider when constructing your resume.

3. Understand the differences between chronological, skills (functional), combination, and online resumes.

4. Learn about the use of key words when computer scanners (OCRs) are used to evaluate resumes.

5. Practice evaluating resumes and using a resume checklist.

6. Organize information for your resume.

7. Understand the importance of assembling a portfolio, learn what an effective portfolio contains, and begin to organize one for yourself.

8. Create a personal web page.

One of the most utilized tools in your **communication toolbox** during the interviewing process is your resume.

You may be asking yourself: "Why do I need a resume? I'm going to work in an office or shop. I'll just go in and show this employer what I can do, hands on." Research has shown, however, that employers want to hire people who have taken the time to prepare a well-organized resume. Remember, the purpose of the resume is not to get a job, but to get you in the door for a job interview. Your resume should represent an honest, accurate presentation of your unique skills, abilities, training, education, and work history.

Many employers say they want to hire employees with effective communication skills, so you need to focus your resume on any **special** communication training you have received. Be sure to study the employers' survey at the end of Chapter One to determine which communication skills employers want to hear potential employees discuss.

This chapter also explains how to assemble a portfolio in order to display visual examples of your skills.

2.1 ORGANIZING RESUME INFORMATION

How do you begin to assemble information when constructing a resume? Study the following resume worksheet for Dave Jessup, and then record your personal information on the blank worksheet pages following Jessup's.

Study this sample resume worksheet.

Resume Worksheet

NAME (in caps) _____ DAVE JESSUP _____

Address _____ W. 504 Hammer Avenue _____

Town, State, Zip _____ Newton, KS 67114 _____

Phone _____ (316) 743-5607 _____

EDUCATION: Institution _Hutchison Community College, Newton, KS_ _____

Year _____ 1996 _____

Degree _____ Currently enrolled, Associate in Applied Science ___

Major _____ Sheet Metal _____

Certificate—Welding 1990 _____

EXPERIENCE:

Dates _1990–Present_ Job Title _____ Welder ___

Company _____ A to Z Welding and Repair _____

Complete Address _205 S. Harrison,_ _____

Newton, KS 67114 _____

Phone _____ (316) 284-6240 _____

Skills/Duties _____ Welding all positions MIG and TIG _____

Dates _1970–1990_ Job Title _____

Company _____ US Air Force _____

Complete Address _Various bases_ _____

Phone _____

Skills/Duties _____ Supervisor of flight mechanics performing _____

maintenance on aircraft electrical, hydraulic, _____

utility and flight control systems. _____

29

Dates _____ Job Title _____

Company _____

Complete Address _____

Phone _____

Skills/Duties _____

EQUIPMENT OPERATED: MIG, TIG, drill press punches, cold saws, drill press,

punches, fork lifts, computers

SPECIAL QUALIFICATIONS   Accounting, fire service rescue, human communication,

industrial first aid, Air Force NCO Academy, supervisor

PROFESSIONAL MEMBERSHIP: _____

_____

_____

MILITARY SERVICE: 20 years

COMMUNITY SERVICE: Cub Scouts, Cubmaster

HOBBIES/INTEREST: Bowling

HONORS/AWARDS: Outstanding NCO 1990 Griffis AFB, Rome, NY

CAREER GOAL (Optional): _____

PERSONAL INFORMATION: Committed to quality control

REFERENCES: At least **THREE,** include name, position, complete address, phone.

1. Name   Jim Math

Position   Shop Foreman

Company   Jim's Fabrication

Work Address   S. 463 Holly St.

Peabody, KS
City   State   Zip

Work Phone (area code)   564-4733

Copyright © 1999 by Allyn and Bacon.

2. Name   Paul Johnson

Position   Owner

Company   Johnson Steel Bldg.

Work Address   N. 5834 River St.

     Salina,   KS

     City   State   Zip

Work Phone (area code)   563-0997

3. Name   Brian Smith

Position   Welding Instructor

Company   Hutchison Community College

Work Address   1500 V. Boyd

     Newton,   KS   67114

     City   State   Zip

Work Phone (area code)   (316) 284-6240

Please note the final resume that was developed from this worksheet on pages 56 and 57. Now complete the following resume worksheet for yourself.

Resume Worksheet

Instructions

The worksheet is for you to use to begin collecting and organizing information for your resume. **This is not a final form,** but it does list several different categories for you to consider. You may not need all of them. Your resume should look *quite different* from the worksheet when you finish it. **Remember,** when writing about your education and work experience, the most current information is *always* listed first.

NAME (in caps) _____

Address _____

Town, State, Zip _____

Phone _____

EDUCATION: Institution _____   Year _____

　　　　　　　　 Degree _____   Major _____

EXPERIENCE:

Dates _____   Job Title _____

　　　　　　　　　　　 Company _____

　　　　　　　　　　　 Complete Address _____

　　　　　　　　　　　 Phone_____

　　　　　　　　　　　 Skills/Duties _____

Dates _____   Job Title _____

　　　　　　　　　　　 Company _____

　　　　　　　　　　　 Complete Address _____

　　　　　　　　　　　 Phone_____

　　　　　　　　　　　 Skills/Duties _____

Dates _____   Job Title _____

　　　　　　　　　　　 Company _____

　　　　　　　　　　　 Complete Address _____

　　　　　　　　　　　 Phone_____

　　　　　　　　　　　 Skills/Duties _____

　　　　　　　　Copyright © 1999 by Allyn and Bacon.

EQUIPMENT OPERATED:_____

SPECIAL QUALIFICATIONS:_____

PROFESSIONAL MEMBERSHIP:_____

MILITARY SERVICE: _____

COMMUNITY SERVICE: _____

HOBBIES/INTERESTS: _____

HONORS/AWARDS: _____

CAREER GOAL (Optional): _____

PERSONAL INFORMATION: _____

REFERENCES: At least **THREE.** Include name, position, address, phone.

1. Name_____

    Position _____

    Company_____

    Work Address _____

City	State	Zip	Work Phone (area code)

2. Name_____

    Position _____

    Company_____

    Work Address _____

City	State	Zip	Work Phone (area code)

3. Name_____

    Position _____

    Company_____

    Work Address _____

City	State	Zip	Work Phone (area code)

2.2 GUIDELINES FOR CONSTRUCTING RESUMES

Resumes usually follow standard formats, yet tell something about you as an individual. A resume reflects what makes you different from other applicants. Employers in business and technical fields often receive so many resumes that they may take only 30 to 90 seconds to glance at a resume, so **be sure** your resume is unique, neat, concise, easy to read, and error-free. Use the following guidelines to accomplish this task:

- Use good-quality paper.
- Try to fit your resume on one page.
- The maximum length is usually two pages for an entry-level position. Time is money to employers, and they do not have the time to read lengthy resumes.
- The exception to the two-page maximum length for resumes would occur if you have a long and varied work history. In this situation, you should limit your employment history to the last ten years unless an earlier job is relevant to the present opening. Even in this case, be as brief as possible.
- If you have a multiple-page resume, be sure to put your name at the top of each page, as in the examples on pages 50 and 52. You do not want an employer to lose or be confused about a critical part of your information.
- Employment gaps? If you have some gaps in your employment record due to an injury, illness, or some other significant event, you can use a short summary paragraph, as in the resume on page 58, to account for this period of time.
- Many different jobs? The same paragraph format can be used for a series of short-term jobs or summer employment.
- How about word usage for the resume? Use active words like those you checked on page 9 in Chapter One. Omit personal pronouns (*I, me, my*), but use short, dynamic phrases and sentences. Fragmented sentences are even permissible to use in a resume.
- Are you a woman with little paid work experience? If you are a woman joining the work force after raising a family, be sure to look at the resume on pages 58 and 59. All that volunteer work with the Cub Scouts and PTA does count!
- Are references necessary? At the end of the resume, job applicants often use the phrase, "References sent upon request." In today's competitive job market, *many* employers prefer to have the references sent **with** the resume, either listed at the end of the resume or attached on a separate sheet of paper. Put your name at the top of your reference page so your resume does not get confused with another applicant's. Because time is money, the interviewer's first choice is usually to find out about applicants *prior to* the interview, rather than having to take the extra time for additional contacts with you and, subsequently, your references.
- Can't type? If a computer keyboard is foreign territory for you, there are firms that will put your resume on a disk for a fee. However, if you collect your own information to construct your resume, it will be much easier to answer questions during an interview because you are very familiar with the data you included in your resume.

Is the focus of your resume important?

How badly do you want this position? You may want to tailor your resume to a specific employment situation. The investment of extra time could be worthwhile because employers often are impressed by the added effort you put into producing a resume relevant to their specific company.

A well-constructed, error-free, easy-to-read resume says a great deal about you. It is worth investing time in your future to build one. But *never* send a resume without a cover letter. An *original* cover letter discussing the unique functions and needs of that prospective employer should accompany each resume. "The basic function of the cover letter is to make the reader curious enough to read the resume," states John Adams, director of career services at Washington State University. "And the resume's real function is simply to make them [employers] curious enough to want to meet you" (Turner B1). Different types of cover letters will be discussed in the next chapter.

Once you have completed the resume worksheet, you need to decide which type of resume you want to develop—a chronological, skills (functional), or combined format. You might also want to explore the possibility of putting your resume on the Internet.

2.3 TYPES OF RESUMES

There are two traditional types of resumes. The **chronological** resume lists your education and work experience according to dates, with the most current information always listed first. Note the examples of these on pages 40–53.

The **skills** (functional) or assets type of resume analyzes your unique skills and abilities according to categories. This type of resume usually does not include previous employers. This format can be useful if you are changing career fields, have a minimal employment record, or have employment gaps. Some employers prefer this style, but others consider it to be too vague. See examples on pages 56–59.

Another type of resume combines these methods of organization. The **combination** resume contains both functional and chronological information. It focuses on your skills and explains how and where you demonstrated using them. A number of employers believe this format is the best. For an example of this style turn to pages 63–64.

A more recent approach to resume writing is an **online resume.** This type of resume, like the more familiar styles, will not get you a job, but it could get you an interview. When preparing information for the Internet, you will need to use a different format. An online resume has a wider and faster distribution to employers and can be more objective than other kinds. Sometimes the online resume is scanned by an optical character reader (OCR) rather than a real person. You can usually use your regular resume to select some key words that are important when designing your resume to go online.

Some of the key words noticed by employers who utilize resume scanning software are:

Ability to delegate	Industrious
Ability to plan	Open communication
Accurate	Organizational skills
Adaptable	Problem solving
Communication skills	Results-oriented
Detail-minded	Safety-conscious
Follow instructions	Team building
High energy	

(Kennedy & Morrow, 2)

Ken Smith, coordinator of the Hotel and Restaurant Management program at Colorado State University, compares an online resume to a traditional resume in this way.

Traditional versus Online

To explain online resumes, it may be better to compare them with the standard resume:

Standard Resume	Electronic Resume
1. Should be grammatically perfect and free of typographical errors.	1. Should be free of typographical errors—the computer does not scan for errors.
2. Centered, with good black print and balanced white space all around.	2. Use sans serif fonts (like Helvetica as in this sentence); avoid complex layouts.* (See below.)
3. Highlight with bolding, underlining, and italics.	3. No boldface, script underlines, or lines of any kind.
4. Concise—one page usually is enough.	4. One page is still good for recent grads; if it goes to two pages, however, it will increase the number of key words and, therefore, the chance of being selected.
5. State your professional objective.	5. Forget the objective, as such; instead use a key word summery.
6. Use full spellings for all words.	6. Abbreviations and industry buzz-words are acceptable.
7. Pack the resume with "action words."	7. Use **key words** throughout.

(18)

An example of an electronic resume is provided on page 66.

A list of E-mail addresses for businesses representing various careers is included in Chapter Three.

Before you mail a resume or put it online, it will be beneficial to your job search if you access a company's web page to find out if the company has a preferred resume format. Some companies will include this information and even describe job openings on their web page.

WORLD OF WORK   Currently, the Boeing Company, with operations in forty states, has a predesigned, fill-in-the-blanks computer resume format for applicants, whether or not a position is available (Internet, May 1997).

Internet company research can be a vital part of your employment exploration because new requirements are constantly emerging. Do not limit your computer inquiries to large corporations; many smaller companies are currently online. If this information is available, it can help you make the decision about which resume format to choose.

---

*Dr. Mary Ellen Guffey suggests using 10- to 14-point Times Roman type because touching letters or unusual fonts are likely to be misread. For the same reason, she says to avoid double columns (*Business Communication News*, 1).

2.4 CHOOSING YOUR RESUME FORMAT

Look at the sample resumes in this section. You may want to follow one of these formats or combine parts of different resumes as a model for your resume. Each format is unique, but each has different strengths and weaknesses. All of the resumes were originally developed by students; only the names, addresses, telephone numbers, and other identifying details have been changed.

Some employers may use an evaluation form like the one on page 71 to rate the resumes they receive, so study that form to determine what could be included in yours.

After examining the resumes to see which styles best fit your background and training, use one or a combination of two or three as a basis for your first draft. A well-crafted resume is a valuable tool to utilize in the paperwork part of getting a job. However, the well-crafted resume cannot be completed in one, two, or even three sessions. Just as building a house involves a multistep process because there is much activity that takes place between floor plans and finish work, resume building is also a multistep process.

When the first printed draft is complete, refer to the resume checklist on pages 68 and 69 to look for areas that need to be added or revised. Often it will be beneficial to have others do some editing of the various drafts just to see if something has been omitted. It is usually necessary to complete **at least three** working drafts after finishing the resume worksheet before sending the final version to an employer.

It is also a good idea to develop different styles of resumes. You may want to send a second application to the same company, or perhaps a particular style will better fit the job description in an advertisement. It will be useful to have chronological, skills, and online resumes in your files, as well as on a computer disk. Always have a backup disk stored in a separate location in case the first disk is misplaced or goes bad.

WORLD OF WORK   A student's backpack was stolen from her car. The backpack contained her disk, backup disk, and the *only* printed copy of her work. She had no other option but to start over from the beginning. Lesson learned? Store your backup disk in a separate location, and save yourself a lot of repetitious work.

CHRONOLOGICAL RESUMES

TED MCDERMONT
Box 3756
Spokane, WA 47385
(647) 766-8685

OBJECTIVE

To obtain a position in the computer industry utilizing training and experience.

EDUCATION

SPOKANE COMMUNITY COLLEGE

North 1810 Greene Street, Spokane, WA 99207. Will graduate with an Associate in Applied Science degree in Computer Programming, 1998.

WORK EXPERIENCE

1992–1996

IVX INDUSTRY, 37251 "A" Street, Seattle, WA 56345. Quality control, responsible for checking quality of computer packaging and parts.

1991–1992

REDDING COMPUTERS, 7456 Harvard, Spokane, WA 97560. Computer sales, purchase orders, maintenance of keyboards.

1990–1991

LEE KEYBOARDS, 45673 Black, Spokane, WA 68699. Keyboard assembly, minor repairs.
Career Path Services

LEADERSHIP

STUDENT AWARENESS LEAGUE,
Elected President 1996–1998
Treasurer 1996–1997
Spokane Community College

AWARDS

STUDENT AWARENESS LEAGUE,
Outstanding Achievement Award for the number one club of the year.

REFERENCES

MATT GENNER
Computer Programming Instructor
Spokane Community College
North 1810 Greene Street
Spokane, WA 99207
(509) 563-6734

MELISSA NEWMAN
Office Technology Instructor
Spokane Community College
North 1810 Greene Street
Spokane, WA 99207
(509) 563-6734

ANGELA WHITE
Speech Communication Instructor
Spokane Community College
North 1810 Greene Street
Spokane, WA 99207
(509) 563-6734

MICHAEL M. KANNEGAARD
East 4785 Tenth Avenue
Spokane, Washington 68567
(567) 759-4756

JOB OBJECTIVES:

Obtain a position in the electronics field with opportunity for advancement to a management position.

EDUCATION:

Winter Quarter 1996 to Present, Spokane Community College, Spokane, Washington
Major ELECTRONICS
Areas of studies completed: DC and AC Theory, Active Devices and Fundamentals of Amplifiers, IC Concepts Both Linear and Digital, Digital Systems Both Hardware and Software.

Fall Quarter 1995, Spokane Community College, Spokane, Washington
Major: Liberal Arts

1970–1991: Attended various military training schools.

EMPLOYMENT HISTORY:

1993–1995   Guard Security Services
Position: General Manager   Spokane, Washington
Duties: Supervised office, sales, and guard personnel. Periodically performed roving and stationary security patrols.

1991–1993   Tractor and Equipment Company
Position: Field Mechanic/Power   Spokane, Washington
                Generation Technician
Duties: Troubleshooting and repair of generators and diesel engines on oil drilling rigs.

1990–1991   USCGC Sunnyview WJL 473
Position: Chief Engineer   Duluth, Minnesota
Duties: Supervising the engineering department. Administering the operating budget. Implemented the preventative maintenance program.

1988–1990   USCGC Confidence EMEI 573
Position: Assistant Chief Engineer Dokiak, Alaska
Duties: Responsible for the electrical and structural repair divisions. Preparing training plans for personnel, including training in electrical/electronics troubleshooting.

PRIOR POSITIONS: Maintenance, repair electrician on various Coast Guard and Navy units, from 1970 to 1988.

MICHAEL M. KANNEGAARD

SPECIAL PROJECTS: Field Sports Director at Boy Scout Camp, Newport, Washington.

Managed the Enlisted Men's Club at the Coast Guard Base in Seattle, Washington.

Operated the Fleet Post Office, Iwo Jima, Japan, 1971.

REFERENCES:

Shelly Links
East 8578 Happy Road
Spokane, Washington 58467
(567) 574-4756
Position: Gerontologist Specialist

Dean C. Kane
North 1810 Greene Street
Spokane, Washington 99207
(574) 586-7844
Position: Electronics Instructor

Don Smith
North 5783 East Street
Spokane, Washington 57467
(574) 566-5680
Position: Boy Scout Executive

Frank James
N. 58463 Sunny Drive
Roswell, NM 57463
(505) 584-8068

CAREER GOALS

To improve machinist skills and move into tool and die work.

EDUCATION

Associate in Applied Science degree as a machinist, Industrial First Aid

1998—Roswell Community College, Roswell, New Mexico. Machine Shop, Shop Math, Blue Print Reading, knowledge in Metallurgy, Drilling, Lathe Operating, Milling, Grinding, Digital Readout experience, and knowledge of CNC programming and operating.

1994—Graduated from Roswell High School, Roswell, New Mexico.

EMPLOYMENT

June 1995–Present	Gibler Tool and Die Production work machining 100 to 1200 parts at a time. Hardinge Automatic Chucker experience, Hardinge Manual Chucker experience, and Bridgeport Mill work.
March 1994–June 1995	Perfect Grinding and Tool Duties: Sharpen End Mills, Shell Mills, Roughing Cutters, Saws, Drills, Step Drills, Center Drills, 135° Split Point Drills and Taps.
June 1993–March 1994	Camp Chevrolet Duties: Put away stock orders, ship parts, and other miscellaneous duties.

HOBBIES

Fishing, Archery Hunting, and Camping.

REFERENCES

Keith Lane	Jim Johnson	Darrin Wines
Machine Shop, Instructor	Machine Shop, Instructor	Gibler Tool & Die
Roswell Community College	Roswell Community College	S. 790 Houk
N. 610 Broad Street	N. 610 Broad Street	Roswell, NM 57463
Roswell, NM 57463	Roswell, NM 57463	(505) 574-0534
(505) 567-8934	(505) 567-893-2122	

DAVE C. HIGHLOW

Current Address	Permanent Address
5745 E. 8th	2674 N. Houk
Spokane, WA 45673	Colville, WA 75673
(573) 456-6778	(574) 684-5746

CAREER GOALS: To perform technical and mechanical evaluation of fluid power components, eventually advancing into sales and outside troubleshooting.

EDUCATION: Will graduate from Spokane Community College, June 1998, with an Associate in Applied Science degree in Fluid Power Technology.

WORK EXPERIENCE: Associated with large-scale family farming operation. Service and repair of all types of farm-related equipment. Also involved in budgeting and accounting functions.

EQUIPMENT OPERATED: Combines, wheel tractors, and large trucks.

LEADERSHIP: Associated Student Council Representative, Spokane Community College, Spokane, WA, 1996–Present. Student Body President, Colville High School, Colville, WA, 1992–1993.

AWARDS: Voted Having Most School Spirit, 1992–1993
Perfect Attendance, 1991–1992

REFERENCES:

John Crocker

Chairman, Fluid Power Department
Spokane Community College
N. 1810 Greene Street
Spokane, WA 99207
(509) 536-7118

Tom White

Teacher and Rancher
Colville High School
Colville, WA 75673
(574) 785-5745

Gary Smith

Teacher and Rancher
Colville High School
Colville, WA 75673
(574) 574-7986

Travis B. Schimmels
E. 57453 Sixth
Spokane, Washington 86743
Telephone (563) 574-3912

Career Goals

To use pipe welding skills and work in the space program.

Education

Will graduate March 1998 from Spokane Community College, Spokane, Washington, with a certificate in welding technology.

Special Studies

MIG, TIG, BLACK IRON TIG, ALUMINUM TIG, DOU SHIELD, BLUEPRINT READING, INDUSTRIAL FIRST AID

Work Experience

7/10/1994–9/14/1994   Steel of Spokane
    Duties—Grinder
3/1991–5/1991   Storey Manufacturing
    Duties—Preparing parts for painting
10/1980–10/1989   Idaho Cascade—Spokane Plywood
    Duties—Offbore and graded veneer, drove forklift, supervised 12 people, ran 3 dryers

Hobbies

Motorcycles, Water skiing

Special Qualities
    Quick hand–eye coordination, fast learner, teachable, honest, dependable

References

Mr. JOE SMITH
    Instructor, Welding Dept.
    Spokane Community College
    N. 1810 Greene Street
    Spokane, WA 99207
    Telephone (509) 845-4836

Mr. DAVE LONGLEGS
    Retired, Kaiser Aluminum
    Truck Farmer
    E. 56734 Indiana
    Greenacres, WA 67897
    Telephone (456) 573-7098

Mr. DAVE JONES
    Foreman
    Idaho Cascade—Spokane Plywood
    Spokane Warehouse Park
    Spokane, WA 85634
    Telephone (597) 780-5008

KIM ROBERTS
S. 496 Rollins Rd.
Greenacres, WA 45785
(574) 866-6999

CAREER GOALS:

To obtain an Electronic Technician position applying current training in Electronic Technology. With increased education and work experience, future goal is to achieve Electrical Engineering position.

EDUCATION:

Will graduate from Spokane Community College, Spokane, WA, with an Associate in Applied Science Degree as a Master Technician. Seven-quarter course involving 50% of classroom time spent on the bench.

Special Courses:

AC and DC theory with linear applications including designing, circuit analysis, schematics, calculations, and troubleshooting. Digital-Computer programming of the Intel 80x86 family of microprocessors. Troubleshooting software and hardware. Interfacing other family devices and other systems to the 80x86 system.

Attended Gonzaga University, Spokane, WA

WORK EXPERIENCE:

Fabric House
E. 48346 Main
Spokane, WA 47363
(367) 484-9090
Position: Responsible for daily reports, which include closing tills at night, making the bank deposit, getting ready for the next business day, inventory, stocking merchandise, checking in orders, customer service.
July 1995–Present

Radio Shack
E. 47363 Clark Avenue
Spokane, WA 47838
(463) 463-9976
Position: Customer service, handling money, stocking, inventory, checking in shipments, pricing, answering telephone.
November 1994–July 1995

8876 Realty
4733 W. 19th Avenue #578
Anchorage, Alaska 47467
(904) 473-6895
Position: Typing, filing, opening mail, answering telephone, handling money, placing newspaper ads, customer relations.
Seasonal July 1994–August 1994

Ruff Restaurant
Old Doggie Way
Anchorage, Alaska 47834
Position: Cashier, answering telephone, preparing salad bar and other food preparation, opening and
closing the store.
Seasonal June 1994–July 1994

Spokane Community College
Bowling Alley
N. 1810 Greene Street
Spokane, WA 99207
(457) 678-4834
Position: Handling money, supervising work-study crew, preparing work schedule, mechanical work in
the alley machines, answering telephone, customer service.
Seasonal September 1992–June 1993; September 1993–June 1994

Empire Insurance Associates, Inc.
E. 4736 Broad
Spokane, WA 73463
(578) 574-0998
Position: Answering telephone, filing, typing, accounting, dealing with clients, opening the office, mag
card.
Seasonal June 1993–September 1993

OUTSIDE INTERESTS:
Snow skiing, bowling, softball, ice and roller skating, sewing.

REFERENCES:

Mrs. Sherry Connell
N. 3673 Ashley Road
Spokane, WA 34633
(473) 574-1123
Friend

Kairi Cougar
Fabric House
E. 48346 Main
Spokane, WA 47363
(367) 484-9090
Supervisor

Mr. Gene Pullman
Spokane Community College
N. 1810 Greene Street
Spokane, WA 99207
(473) 354-0087
Electronics Instructor

ROB JORDAN
456 N. 2nd Street
Colville, Washington 36322
(767) 846-3482

CAREER GOALS

To obtain a position in the electronics industry to utilize skills learned as an electronic technician.

EDUCATION

Associate in Applied Science degree in Electronics, Spokane Community College, Spokane, WA
Seven quarter course including: AC/DC theory, basic and advanced theory, semiconductors, active and passive devices, and special courses.

SPECIAL COURSES

Communications: AM and FM theory, receivers, transmitters, and troubleshooting.

Microwave: Microwave theory, PC board construction, terrestrial links, satellite television, and troubleshooting fiber optics.

Digital Systems: Microprocessor theory, printers, storage, data communications, using various software.

Data Processing: Microprocessor theory, printers, storage, data communications, using various software.

BASIC Programming: Writing programs using the BASIC language.

LICENSES AND CERTIFICATES

FCC General Class License
Washington State Master's Certificate of Electronic Technology
Job Communication Skills

EMPLOYMENT

Department of Natural Resources
 Summer 1996, 1995
Duties: Building and maintenance of off road vehicle trail, forest fire suppression, operation and maintenance of vehicles.

Spokane Community College, Electronics Department
 1993–1994 school year
Duties: Troubleshooting, calibration, and repair of equipment used in the department.

John James Ranch
Summer 1991, 1992, 1993
Duties: Care of show horses and cattle, equipment operation, maintenance and repair, fence repair, hay and grain hauling using various 2 ton trucks.

INTERESTS

Motorcycles, four-wheel driving, fishing, flying, snowmobiles, hunting, radio control planes and boats, and learning more about the field of electronics.

REFERENCES

Jim Heinz
Microwave Instructor
Spokane Community College
North 1810 Greene Street
Spokane, WA 99207
(586) 574-0000 Ext. 12945

Jay Braus
Digital Systems Instructor
Spokane Community College
North 1810 Greene Street
Spokane, WA 99207
(586) 574-0000 Ext. 17345

Meagan New
Department of Natural Resources
ORV Crew Supervisor
(Home address) 463 South Ash
Spokane, WA 47343
(456) 463-1234

Monty Gains
Instructional Technician
Spokane Community College
North 1810 Greene Street
Spokane, WA 99207
(586) 574-0000 Ext. 1798

Mark Hines
Department of Natural Resources
Northeast Area Supervisor
Northeast Area Headquarters
Colville, WA 46733
(645) 464-5785

GARY M. JONES
East 8367 10th
Spokane, WA 87665
(836) 684-4857

OBJECTIVE:

To obtain a position in the automotive field where training and experience can be immediately and profitably utilized by the employer.

EDUCATION:

Spokane Community College, North 1810 Greene Street, Spokane, WA 99207
Degree: Associate in Applied Science, Automotive Technology, March 1995
Courses: Engine and Chassis Electrical, Air Conditioning, Tune-Up, Brakes, Front End and Suspension, Engines and Transmissions
Electives: Welding, Basic Electronics, Industrial First Aid, Job Communication Skills

SPECIAL QUALIFICATIONS:

Certified in Automotive Service Excellence, State Emission Specialist

WORK EXPERIENCE:
1994–present

Cars East, East 57346 Lane Street, Spokane, WA 57363
Mechanic: Responsible for repairs and diagnosis on all makes and models of vehicles.

1992–1994

Tommy's Auto Wrecking, South 4783 Creek, Spokane, WA 57846
Yardman: Responsible for removal of auto parts, inventory and stocking, sales, and delivery.

1989–1991

Self-employed mechanic, South 567 9th Street, Yakima, WA 88673
Operated small shop, performed repairs on automobiles and farm equipment.

1986–1988

Bob C. White Farms, Route 2, Box 98, Yakima, WA 58474
Farm worker: Operated and repaired farm equipment on a large-scale wheat ranch.

1980–1985

Paul D. Crow Construction, East 4736, Yakima, WA 57467
Truck driver: Also operated backhoe, front-end loader, D-6 cat, and road grader.

INTERESTS:

Fishing, reading, cars

REFERENCES:

Tommy D. Long
Owner
Tommy's Auto Wrecking,
South 4783 Creek
Spokane, WA 57846
(567) 448-5847 (Work)
(567) 847-7846 (Home)

Don Perry
Instructor
Spokane Community College
North 1810 Greene Street
Spokane, WA 99207
(674) 678-5784

Bernie C. Loud
Parts Manager
Tommy's Auto Wrecking
South 4783 Creek,
Spokane, WA 57846
(567) 448-5847 (Work)
(567) 847-7846 (Home)

SCOTT B. SHAY
67563 E. BLACK RD
ELK, WA 84573
(674) 474-7836

CAREER GOALS

To become skilled at maintenance and troubleshooting using past experience and current training as a fluid power technician.

WORK EXPERIENCE

1993–Present

Sears Automotive, 674 Division, Spokane, WA.
Automotive Parts Installer. Responsible for installing and repairing automotive equipment.

1983–1992

United States Navy, Aviation Machinist Mate First Class.
Quality Control Inspector. Responsible for final inspection of all downing or serious discrepancies.

Supervised Powerplant Shops on four different types of aircraft. Responsible for maintenance and inspection of aircraft.

Flight Line Supervisor for three different types of aircraft. Responsible for all ground handling of aircraft.

Calendar Inspection Crew Supervisor.
Responsible for all in-depth inspections and parts replacement on aircraft.

Fuel Crew Supervisor. Responsible for fueling aircraft, accounting for fuel, and maintenance of trucks and equipment.
Crews supervised: 5 to 25 military personnel.

Specialized Military Training:
    Leadership and Management School.
    Quality Assurance Administration School.
    Aircraft Systems Schools on five different aircraft.
    Complete Engine Overhaul School on two different engines.

ORGANIZATIONS

Member of Society of Manufacturing Engineers, Spokane Community College, Student Chapter.

Member of the Spokane Skydivers.

HOBBIES

Dog training, camping

REFERENCES

Don Carl
Automotive Service Manager
Sears Automotive Center
674 Division
Spokane, WA 89674
(456) 560-5746

John Day, Chairman
Fluid Power Department
Spokane Community College
N. 1810 Greene Street
Spokane, WA 99207
(546) 456-1543

Gary White, Engineer
Boeing
S. 47846 Brown Street
Spokane, WA 58746
(466) 755-4412

SKILLS RESUMES

DAVE J. JESSUP
W. 504 Hammer Ave.
Newton, KS 67114
(346) 743-5607

WORK EXPERIENCE

Shielded Metal Arc Welding . . . Gas Metal Arc Welding (M.I.G.) . . . Gas Tungsten Arc Welding (T.I.G.) Black Iron & Aluminum . . . Air Carbon Arc . . . Plasma Arc . . . Iron Worker . . . Drill Press . . . Band Saws . . . Cold Saws . . . Overhead Cranes . . . Fork Lifts . . . Measuring Devices . . . Grinders . . . Assorted Power Machines, Punches, Saws, Shears, Breaks, Tools & Equipment . . . Blueprint, Schematic & Diagram Reading . . . Inspection . . . Computer Operation . . . Quality Control . . . Stock & Inventory . . . Helicopter Maintenance

EDUCATIONAL BACKGROUND

Presently enrolled in the Industrial Sheet Metal course at Hutchison Community College, Newton, Kansas.

Graduated December 1990, from Hutchison Community College, with a certificate in Welding Technology.

FORMAL AND TECHNICAL

- Industrial Welding
- Basic College Accounting Fundamentals
- Basic Computer Application and Literacy
- Industrial Safety and First Aid
- Human Communications
- Management for Air Force Supervisors
- Aircraft Maintenance Management
- Base Level Supply Management
- Air Force NCO Academy
- Advanced Helicopter Technical Training
- Helicopter Gas Turbine Engine Systems
- Helicopter Transmission and Drive Systems
- Aircraft Electrical Systems
- Aircraft Hydraulic and Utility Systems
- Aircraft Flight Control Systems
- Helicopter Fundamentals
- Aircraft Structures
- Aircraft Maintenance Fundamentals
- Fire Service Rescue

CAREER HIGHLIGHTS

Welder

October 1990–Present
Cut, punched, drilled, fit, and welded metal components in the fabrication of steel structures and assemblies.

UNITED STATES AIR FORCE   1965–1990

Maintenance Management Supervisor

Directed, coordinated, and monitored helicopter maintenance production activities. Compiled and maintained computer files consisting of inspection schedules, maintenance and supply requirements.

Deputy Commander for Maintenance

Provided overall management and supervision of 25 helicopter maintenance and support personnel, aircraft, equipment, and facilities.

Transient Alert Branch Supervisor

Managed 20 personnel, providing services and maintenance for all transient aircraft.

Helicopter Branch Supervisor and Flight Mechanic

Supervised 12 mechanics and their related activities. Diagnosed and solved maintenance problems. Planned and scheduled work procedures.

Helicopter Mechanic

Performed as maintenance crew chief, troubleshooting, repairing, inspecting, and servicing aircraft and equipment. Maintained forms and records, initiated supply transactions, and coordinated specialist support.

REFERENCE

Jim Math	Paul Johnson	Brian Smith
Shop Foreman	Owner	Welding Instructor
Jim's Fabrication	Johnson Steel Bldg.	Hutchison Community
S. 463 Holly St.	N. 5834 River St.	College
Peabody, KS 44777	Harp, KS 47377	1500 N. Boyd
(913) 564-4733	(913) 563-0997	Newton, KS 67114
		(316) 284-6240

WILKS, DEBRA J.
East 567 3rd Street
Rome, NY 74733

Telephone 584-0023

CURRENT
EXPERIENCE
1978–1998

<u>Mother and wife:</u>
Skills developed raising four self-reliant children and maintaining home include: counselor, teacher, nurse, financial adviser, hostess, decorator, cook, chauffeur, social secretary. Qualities contributing to congenial home life are:

> adaptability, effective organization, ability to cope under stress and make quick decisions, alertness to needs of others, rapport with all age groups, ingenuity, and sense of humor.

WORK-RELATED SKILLS

<u>Volunteer work:</u>

Board member, Rome Symphony Women's Association, 1991–1995. Coordinated with Symphony office staff on promotional advertising, compiled mailings, handled seating requests, planned renewal night for season tickets, 1992–1994; correlated and directed sales campaign for SSWA calendar. Chairman of city-wide rummage sale—netted $16,000; chairperson annual membership luncheon—over 200 members.

Member, Board of Trustees, St. George's School/past president Mother's Guild: Developed better interschool communication; raised $4,000 on cookbook sales/editor of parent's newspaper/team captain annual fund drive.

Member, Board of Trustees, Greater Rome Music and Allied Arts Festival, 1990 to present. Chairman of dance division: Schedule classes, hire adjudicator, establish scholarships.

COMMENDATIONS

General chairperson of various activities including: Church bazaar, style show luncheon, all school carnival, city-wide talent show, receptions, banquets.

Received bronze medal in appreciation for hours of service as tour guide and security guard at Art during Expo.

Elected delegate to National P.E.O. Convention in Boston by Chapter E in appreciation for term as president.

Received commendation for five years of service as Camp Fire leader.

Acknowledged by church for seven years devoted to Sunday school teaching.

EDUCATION

EWSC—1986, art history.
Whitworth College—1986, economics and government.
Stanford University—1971–73, foreign languages.

WORK EXPERIENCE

Secretary for John J. Eck, attorney-at-law, 1973.

Security guard for multi-million-dollar art collection, Art Gallery, Expo.

Employed by Bon Marche for storewide inventory, 1986.

ESTIMATE OF MY POTENTIAL

Am confident that past experience has developed expertise in dealing with people, promoting sales, organizing fund-raising events, and coordinating large functions. Feel qualified to enter the job market in fields related to office management, public relations, convention/ tourist trade, sales promotion. Would consider additional college education with on-the-job training to give maximum performance. Equipped with maturity and imagination to meet challenges.

INTERESTS

Backpacking, gourmet cooking, crocheting, music, and theater.

REFERENCES

Bob E. Ants, Headmaster
St. Kelly's School
West 43 Smith Road
Rome, NY 54389
(315) 589-6987

Mike L. Lanes Jr., Assistant Vice-President
John Lynch, Inc.
West 4734 Main
Rome, NY 47377
(315) 574-5967

George Joggle, Upper School Principal
St. Kelly's School
West 43 Smith Road
Rome, NY 54389
(315) 589-6987

Ginny Red
National committee member, World Service Council
East 473 22nd Avenue
Rome, NY 48488
(315) 347-3840

COMBINATION RESUME

KEITH JAY RIBBLES

North 1984 Collins Road
Hyannis, MA 99456
(781) 987-0976

SUMMARY OF QUALIFICATIONS

- International Representative with strong professional background in labor relations, contract negotiations, arbitration, grievance and dispute resolutions.

- Proven effectiveness in Human Relations, with demonstrated ability to establish rapport quickly, interview effectively, and accurately assess people's needs.

- Excellent communication skills with demonstrated ability to deal successfully with people under stressful situations. Well-developed verbal and written communication skills, with the ability to organize information and write in clear, concise, and easily understood terms.

- Professional, well-organized, disciplined, and persistent, with credible public image and the ability to work effectively in high-pressure environment. Stay calm under stress, respond quickly when required, and develop solutions to problems.

AREAS OF EXPERIENCE

Contract Negotiations	Administrative Law Judge
Grievance Resolution	Hearings
Arbitration	Employees' Seminars
Employment Hearings	Team Negotiations
Interviews	Benefit Trust Member
Seminar Training	

EDUCATION

Currently attending Cape Cod Community College, enrolled in Mid-Management with emphasis on Personnel Management.

Attended Cape Cod Community College, 1984.

Attended Gordon College, Wenham, MA, 1982.

Graduated Bourne High School, Bourne, MA, 1980.

EMPLOYMENT EXPERIENCE

1993–1994   Leasing Manager, Mico Leasing, Woods Hole, MA
Managed over-the-road trailer operations, with responsibility for all day-to-day business decisions, including filing, bookkeeping, record keeping, sales and maintenance, collections, and correspondence.

1990–1992   Special Procedures Technician, Mercy General Hospital, Hyannis, MA
As special procedures technician, duties were to assist in surgery and in emergency room as time permitted.

MILITARY EXPERIENCE

1986–1990   Hospital Corpsman and Independent Duty Specialist, and Survival Medicine Instructor, Hospital Corpsman Fleet, U.S. Marine Force

LEADERSHIP

Elected Secretary, Moose Lodge, Council 8704.

Den leader and pack assistant, Cub Scout, Pack 678.

Hobbies include golf, fishing, and camping.

REFERENCES

Ruth Smith
Director, Early Learning Center
Cape Cod CC
Hyannis, MA 99876
(781) 533-7615

Tom Jones, Auditor
North 3698 8th Road
Hyannis, MA 99876
(781) 385-3475

Todd Kohl
Assistant Division Director
Mico Leasing
3746 65th Southwest
Newton, MA 99876
(781) 473-6784

ONLINE ELECTRONIC RESUME

Summary:
- Relate well to the needs and wants of guests in the hospitality industry.
- Communicate effectively in person and on the telephone.
- Adept in the use of computers.
- Able to acquire business routines rapidly.
- Perform productively under stress.
- Problem solve effectively in emergency situations.

Owen C. Thomas
E. 204 4th Avenue
Bellevue, WA 99023
206-923-1627

Objective: Looking for new horizons, challenges, and opportunities for advancement to management within the hospitality industry, where personal experience can benefit an employer.

Experience:
1994–Present   Front Desk Assistant, Head Bellman
The Bellevue Club, Bellevue, WA
A hundred-year-old private club with two dining rooms, eighty-bed hotel, three bars, and athletic facilities.
- Provide room service for club guests.
- Respond to members requests in person and on the telephone.
- Assist in the bar, espresso machine, kitchen, and/or dining room as needed.
- Responsible for end of shift cash receipts.

1993–1994   Cashier/Work Study
Spokane Community College Culinary Arts Restaurant
- Responsible for guest checks and payments.
- Accountable for all money collected and balanced, with daily computer-generated reports and deposits.

1980–Present   Family Business
Clark Custom Caning and Refinishing
- Supervise employees in restoration of antique and modern furniture.
- Provide repair estimates.
- Schedule pick up and delivery services.
- Sell supplies.
- Record bookkeeping accounts on computer.

Education: Spokane Community College
Associate in Applied Science degree 1994
Hotel Restaurant Management
President's/Vice President's Honor Roll

Certificates: Speech Communication
Applied Food Service Sanitation
Industrial First Aid

References:

Duane Aspen
Front Desk Manager
The Bellevue Club
W. 1002 Ironwood Drive
Bellevue, WA 99023
(206) 416-1100

Richard Gregg, Instructor
Culinary Arts
Orlando's Restaurant
Spokane Community College
N. 1810 Greene St.
Spokane, WA 99207
(509) 533-1027

Bill Plant
Businessman
E. 21824 24th
Kent, WA 99307
(416) 289-1802

Owen C. Thomas
E-mail: othomas@ctc.com

2.5 CHECKING RESUMES

This resume checklist is a helpful tool to use after completing a printed draft of your resume. The checklist can help you identify some additional important information about your background, training, or experience that was mistakenly omitted or is not in the correct resume sequence. The checklist also can serve as a reminder to check for mechanical errors such as misspelled words, mistakes in grammar, and the quality of the paper. Before constructing your own resume, practice using the checklist to evaluate one of the resumes in this chapter in order to gain experience in looking for errors.

TOOLS OF COMMUNICATION

Using the Resume Checklist

Instructions

Turn to the resume on page 45. Use this checklist to rate the format of that resume with either a yes or a no. If the item does not apply, leave the space blank. When you have completed section 7 of this checklist, add the yes and no responses. Compare your score with that of someone else in the class. How close were your ratings for this resume?

_____   1. Resume heading: Does it include name, address, and phone number?

_____   2. Goals or objective (optional):

_____   a. Is the purpose and the type of work desired identified (optional)?

_____   b. Does the resume apply for *work,* not a job title?

_____   c. Career goal (also optional)?

_____   3. Is there appropriate wording for degrees and/or certificates?

_____   a. Associate in Applied Science Degree

_____   b. Associate of Arts Degree

_____   c. Certified Automotive Service Excellence

_____   d. Welding Certificate

_____   e. Certificate in Industrial First Aid

_____   4. Experience: All is good; some is just better than others, and the *most current is always first.*

_____   a. Does work data seem complete—job, title, duties, name of the firm or organization, place, and specific dates?

_____   b. If experience is part-time or work study, is it identified as such?

_____   c. Are skills from page 9 incorporated, and do sentences start with an active verb (like *supervising, directing*)?

_____   d. Are personal pronouns such as *I, me,* and *my* omitted?

_____   e. Sentence fragments are acceptable in resumes—for example, "Loading dock: Supervising five employees." Are active sentences and/or phrases utilized?

_____   f. Are comments such as "This was an outstanding job" avoided? This is a factual report, and such statements are a matter of opinion.

_____   g. Are generalities, such as "honest," "reliable," or "anxious to get ahead" omitted? (Self-appraisal like that can indicate there are no concrete accomplishments to talk about.)

_____ 5. Does this resume pay special attention to mechanics?

_____   a. Is good-quality paper used? **No** perforated paper pages from dot matrix printers should ever be sent to potential employers.

_____   b. Is the resume well written, with no misspelled words or strikeovers, and are any error corrections undetectable?

_____   c. Is punctuation at a minimum but in keeping with grammatical correctness?

_____   d. Are accepted state abbreviations used, such as WA or MA?

_____   e. Is the print dark, laser print or near letter quality, and without smudges?

_____   f. Is it specific? The use of "and so on" or "etc." to end a sentence is too general and a waste of space. Are these omitted?

_____   g. Are salaries omitted?

_____ 6. Personal details may be important to the person you are rating, but to a prospective employer they represent the least relevant information of these qualifications.

_____   a. Are marital status, height, weight, and photographs omitted?

_____   b. Also, it is not necessary to list hobbies and interests if space is at a premium. Is unimportant information omitted?

_____ 7. References should be selected carefully.

_____   a. Are the references' business titles included, so the prospective employer can weigh the significance of the reference?

_____   b. Are the references listed in address form, and do they include all information necessary for the employer to contact that reference—telephone number, too?

_____ 8. Format emphasizes ease of reading and space saving. In your opinion, does this resume contain the main factors affecting the physical arrangement?

_____   a. Does the resume have attractive form and placement?

_____   b. Are the lines single spaced within the paragraphs, and is double spacing used between the paragraphs?

_____   c. Are the margins $1\frac{1}{2}$ to 2 inches on both left and right sides as well as the top and bottom of each page?

_____   d. Is the material balanced across the page in tabulated form?

_____   e. If an item is carried over to another line, is the second line indented two spaces?

_____   f. Are the main captions in all capitals and/or boldface letters?

_____   g. Does difference in placement show awareness of organizational principles?

_____   h. Does the use of bullets (•) draw attention to important areas?

TOTAL YES RESPONSES _____

TOTAL NO RESPONSES _____

WORLD OF WORK   Is the style of printing on a resume important?

During a preemployment interview, the personnel manager for a robotics company said he will not even *read* a resume if it is printed on perforated paper or from a dot matrix printer.

If you do not have access to a computer when you are constructing your resume, and you *must* use a typewriter, be sure the typewriter keys are clean and the ribbon is fresh. However, putting your resume on a computer disk makes it much easier to update.

2.6 GRADING RESUMES

As was mentioned earlier, some employers use a grading sheet to evaluate resumes in order to determine whom to interview when the resume is mailed to them. Other employers will grade the resume following the interview if they do not see it until that time. Most employers will have some way of ranking resumes, and they often circle keywords or even errors on the resume itself.

You can better understand this grading process if you try using it yourself.

TOOLS OF COMMUNICATION

Grading a Resume

Instructions

Use the resume evaluation form on page 71 to determine how you would grade two resumes from this chapter. Compare your grade with your instructor's grade or that of someone else who has knowledge of resume construction. Was your grade similar to the other person's? This evaluation tool is also useful in ascertaining how employers might evaluate your resume.

RESUME EVALUATION FORM

	Points	Poor	Fair	Good	Excellent
1. What was the overall general appearance of the resume? (40 points)					
2. Did resume use an appropriate format? (15 points)					
3. Were there any mechanical errors (spelling, punctuation, grammar, etc.)? (25 points)					
4. Were there any typographical errors on the resume? (15 points)					
5. Did the resume show the strengths of the potential employee (education, work skills, personal information)? (25 points)					
6. References (3) including name, position, address, phone. (30 points)					

General comments: _____

_____

_____

_____

Your points: _____   Total possible points: ___150___

WORLD OF WORK   An employer for an electrical maintenance company contacted an instructor at the local college to complain about the poor quality and number of mistakes a recent graduate of the electrical program had made on his resume. He went on to say he wouldn't hire anyone who did such sloppy paperwork, no matter how good his or her skills were!

> Remember, "There is wisdom in many counselors," —Solomon.

Feedback from others is very useful. Using copies of that same evaluation form on page 71, ask two people to grade your resume prior to submitting it for a final grade, sending it to prospective employers, or taking it to job interviews. This process can provide useful feedback about the effectiveness of your resume. Others often will discover errors you may have missed because you are so familiar with your own information. Also, it will be useful to have your resume evaluated by at least one person outside of your class but in your career area. When you receive feedback from someone who has knowledge of your training but does not know you personally, that person's rating will probably be more objective.

For another evaluator, select someone completely unfamiliar with your career field to determine if your employment history and training are presented clearly. This feedback is useful when your resume will be evaluated by someone such as a personnel director. You will want to know if this information can be understood by a person who is not familiar with your training.

What else can be done to differentiate yourself from other applicants? Assembling information for a portfolio can be a productive use of your time.

WORLD OF WORK   Following a recent series of interviews for a carpentry position, the journeyman carpenter conducting the interviews asked the interviewees why only *one* out of the four interviewees had taken the time to put together pictures of his work. He stressed that photographs of work in progress and completed work were excellent methods of showing an employer what you have accomplished.

2.7 BUILDING PORTFOLIOS

A *portfolio* is a word often associated with spies like James Bond, diplomats in foreign countries, or artists, not those in technical or business fields. However, anyone can make a very effective use of a portfolio.

A portfolio is a documented, often pictorial record of work that provides a visual demonstration of your specific skills and abilities. This collection of personal accomplishments is something to take with you to show a prospective employer.

How could a portfolio be organized, and what should be included? It works well to purchase a plain, attractive $8\frac{1}{2} \times 11$, three-ring notebook (no hearts, flowers, or company logos) with acetate pages in a variety of pocket sizes.

A portfolio is an ongoing project and could include:

- Photographs of your work, a building you helped to construct, a car that was restored, clothing or hair styles you created
- Samples of projects completed, computer designs you originated, or programs you formed
- A record of presentations in which you participated
- Awards, certificates, or letters of commendation earned
- Copies of projects, flyers, or brochures designed by you
- Any original writing you produced or documents you developed
- Letters of recommendation
- Any self-assessment tools you have used, such as a learning style analysis or a Meyers-Briggs personality profile, to give a potential employer a multidimensional picture of who you are

Once you have collected this unique profile of what you can do and who you are, put it in the notebook in an organized manner. For example, all pictures and samples of your work could go in one section, a record of your awards in another area, and letters of recommendation would be included toward the end. As with a resume, the most current, relevant portfolio information should be first. Number the pages, and then make a table of contents page for the front of the portfolio listing the topics and the page number where each topic begins.

WORLD OF WORK Last year, during a practice interview, a student in the cosmetology department brought a portfolio of her work to show the employer. The employer was very impressed with the photos of the student's fingernail art. In fact, the employer called back to ask the student to come in for a "real" interview. As this situation demonstrates, taking the time to develop a personal portfolio could be very profitable.

2.8 CREATING A WEB PAGE

A recent evolution in the job-seeking market is the creation of a personal web page and an E-mail address on the Internet by those seeking employment. Your web page could include some of the items incorporated in a portfolio. The advantage of an individualized web page is that it can be accessible to a wide range of potential employers.

A color scanner is a useful piece of equipment to help you produce your unique web page. You can use the scanner to format the page to include photographs, designs, certificates, or any of the other items mentioned on page 73 of this chapter, in the section on portfolios.

The existence of your web page and an E-mail address would need to be mentioned in your cover letters.

If you do not know how to develop a web page but believe it would be beneficial, there are those who can teach you how to design one or can produce one for you for a fee. Contact a computer department at your local college or university for this information.

It is important to keep updating your portfolio, your resume, and your web page even *after* getting a position, because you never know when an internal promotion or an opportunity for advancement with another company may occur. With a current resume, an updated portfolio, and a current web page, you will always be ready to take advantage of new opportunities in rapidly changing employment fields.

STRESS LESS   When you have revised your resume for the third time and the instructor says you *still* need to make more corrections, try the following stress-reducing exercises.

The One-Minute Vacation

Picture someplace in the world you would like to be—the woods, the seashore, or a mountaintop. Set a timer, and mentally stay in that picture for one minute. If you can relax for even *one minute,* your stress level will go down.

A variation of this "stress less" exercise is to buy a poster or picture of a favorite scene and use the one-minute break to look at the picture.

CASE STUDY   *Study two resumes in this chapter from different career fields. Thinking of yourself as a personnel interviewer, list the strengths and weaknesses of these resumes. How would you improve them?*

CHAPTER PROJECT   In teams of four or five, study three resumes on pages 40 and 41, 42 and 43, and 58 and 59. Each of you should evaluate them separately, using both the resume checklist and the resume evaluation form. Then, as a team, decide which two people you would call back for an interview. Explain to the rest of the class why you would want to interview these people.

DISCUSSION QUESTIONS

1. What information do you believe is the most important to include in a resume?
2. Which type of resume formats do you think are the most useful? Why?
3. What would you recommend adding to the resume information to make it more meaningful?
4. What would you add to a portfolio and/or web page to make it even more relevant for your career field?

SUMMARY

In this chapter you learned about:

- Different methods and guidelines for organizing information for resumes
- Electronic resumes
- Various resume formats
- Checking and evaluating resumes
- Portfolios and web pages

Armed with this information about yourself, you are ready to research available positions and to prospect for information about companies of interest to you.

CHAPTER THREE

Creating Interest in Yourself

APPLICATION FOR EMPLOYMENT

LEARNING OBJECTIVES

1. Understand the importance of knowing about businesses. Learn how to research them and how to expand your network of employers.

2. Practice using various resources for researching companies.

3. Understand the importance of cover letters and the different types of letters.

4. Learn how to evaluate cover letters and practice evaluating them.

5. Practice writing solicited and unsolicited cover letters.

6. Understand the importance of finishing application forms appropriately. Learn the guidelines for filling them out correctly, and practice completing them accurately.

7. Understand what affirmative action forms may contain.

Have you ever experienced the discomfort of writing to someone you did not know? Did you ever go out on a date with someone you had not met? If so, you will have a sense of what it is like to write a letter to an unknown person in a company, or to go to a job interview and know nothing about the work the company does. To reduce this discomfort, you can research **before** you send a cover letter with your resume or go to a job interview.

You may be interested in working for a specific company in your local area, in another state, or even in a different country. But if this business has not advertised a vacant position for someone with your skills, what can you do to get their attention? Researching the company at a library and/or on the Internet or CD ROM can give you valuable information. This knowledge will help you write a cover letter to them because you will be able discuss their *type of work* accurately and explain how your training could benefit them.

Remember to keep records of all employers that you research and/or contact in the network of employers that you started in Chapter One.

3.1 CREATE INTEREST IN YOURSELF BY THOROUGHLY KNOWING ABOUT A COMPANY BEFORE YOU WRITE TO THEM

Let's explore some channels of information for researching companies. Incidentally, there is an additional benefit for you in doing this research: The information may help you to decide **if** this is the type of company where you want to work.

Getting started with this exploration is sometimes the most challenging part of the job search process. One of the richest sources of information is usually a college or local library. If you will just **ASK** for help, most librarians are eager to assist you.

One useful book is the *Standard Industrial Classification Manual* (SIC Code Manual). This publication, available in most libraries and online, is a numerical classification of all types of technical fields and business establishments. It was developed by the U.S. government to facilitate collection, tabulation, presentation, and analysis of statistical data concerning employers, what they do, and their economic status. Once you determine the SIC code(s) for your career, you can utilize directories such as these:

1. *Thomas Register of American Manufacturers*
2. Dun and Bradstreet's *Million Dollar Directory,* which gives details of both geographical and occupational information
3. *Standard and Poor's Corporation Records,* which contains information on publicly held corporations
4. *Occupational Outlook Handbook*
5. *Moody's Manuals*
6. *U.S. Industrial Outlook* is:
   —Published yearly by the Department of Commerce.
   —Each industry describes the current employment situation, the outlook for next year, and long-term five-year prospects.
7. *Hoover's Handbook of American Business* profiles over 500 major U.S. corporations.
8. Regional publications such as:
   * *Advanced Technology in Washington State*
   * *Washington State Manufacturers Directory*
   * *Oregon Directory of Manufacturers*
   * *Dun's Regional Business Directory*
9. Profiles of specific companies are often available at the library or through the company's personnel office.
10. If you have access to the *American Business* CD ROM disk and the SIC codes relevant to your career field, you can access almost all of the data listed in these various printed sources. In a short span of time, this disk

will allow you to research specific companies in various geographic areas using a computer. It will also give you information concerning the financial status of that company along with the names, addresses and phone numbers of the appropriate contact persons.

Where can you find additional sources of information about companies and positions? You can:

1. Look in both local and out of town newspapers. Read the business section of the papers, as well as the want ads, to identify new trends.
2. Ask your friends for names, and add these names to those you collected in the Chapter One employer's survey project to continue to build a network of information.
3. Write or call the chamber of commerce in a town or city where you want to work. Ask for names of employers in that area who hire people in your career field.
4. Use the direct approach by going to companies and businesses:
   ⇒ Go to personnel offices, sometimes referred to as human resource offices.
   ⇒ Request a tour of the shop or office.
   ⇒ Talk to current employees on their break if possible.
   ⇒ Make an appointment with the lead supervisor or office manager, ask questions and make notes of the answers.
5. Go to career, placement or cooperative education offices on campus.
6. Check state, city, and county offices for advertised openings.
7. Research CD-ROM indexes.
8. Investigate online computer search engines such as Netscape Navigator or Internet Explorer.

9. Several specific computer addresses are listed here for your convenience:

Web Site	*Addresses*
Incorporating the Internet in Your Job Search	www.wpi.edu/depts/
America's Job Bank	www.ajb.dni.us/
E-Span Employment Database	www.esoab.cin
Heart Career Connections	www.career.com
HiTech Careers	www.hitechcareer.com/
Job Center	www.jobcenter.com
Monster Board Career Site	www.monster.com
Jobs Online	www.ceweekly.wa.com
Business Job Finder	www.cob.ohio-state.edu/dept/fin/ osujobs.html
Federal Government Agencies	www.lib.lsu.edu/gov/fedgov.html
Internet Sleuth: Employment	www.charm.net~ibc/sleuth/empl.html
Chicago Tribune Career Finder	www.chicago.tribune.com
FedWorld	www.fedworld.gov
MedSearch America	www.medsearch.com
Workplace	www.galaxy.einet.net/galaxy/ Community/Workplace.html
Electronic Newsstand	www.enews.com
International Careers	www.wm.edu/catapult/interntl.html
National Business Employment Weekly	www.occ.com/occ/NBEW/ NBEWO1.html
Newspapers on the Internet	www.deltanet.com

10. The Commercial Sites Index: www.directory.net

This searchable collection of company and organization pages includes links to more than 20,000 web pages that will aid in exploring specific businesses or industries.

How can you put this information to practical use? Study the following sample job research project to see how to adapt it to your field.

Perhaps you want to move to the Pacific Northwest and are trained as a welder. The SIC numbers for that field are *1799, 7692, 7694, 3715, 3713, 7519, 7539.* The *Thomas Register* of company profiles and the *Thomas Register of Products and Services,* with listings by state and SIC code, lists companies that employ welders. Dun and Bradstreet's 1995 *Million Dollar Directory* of manufacturers, cross-referenced by geography, lists several companies in Spokane, WA. One of those employers is Alloy Trailers, Inc.

Sample Job Research Project

The following is an example of information you would find about Alloy Trailers Inc., in Dun and Bradstreet (136).

D-U-N-S 00-906-5152
ALLOY TRAILERS INC. (WA)
S3025 Geiger Blvd., Spokane, WA 99204
Tel (509) 455-8650   Founded/Ownrshp 1945
Sales 31MM   Emp 300
Bank: Washington Trust Bank, Spokane, WA
Accts: Roger Frucci & Associates

SIC 3715 3713 7539 7519 Truck trailers; Van bodies; Trailer repair; Trailer rental.
* *J Kingsley Novell*   *Ch Bd*
* *Frank Pignanelli*   *Pr*
* *Richard H Peirone*   *Ex VP*
* *Robert K Novell*   *Sec Tr*
* *Frank Gibler*   *VP*
* *Gregory Kreshel*   *VP*
* *Susan Rice*   *VP Comp*

A research information sheet would contain the following data concerning Alloy:

1. *Name of Company:* Alloy Trailers, Inc.
2. *Address: S. 3025 Geiger Blvd. Spokane, WA 99204.*
3. *Phone number: (509) 455-8650, Fax: (509) 747-4811*
4. *Contact person: Frank Pignanelli, Pres. (or call to find person who does the hiring).*
5. *Type of work: Truck trailers, van bodies*
   Trailer repair and rental
6. *Additional Company Information: In business since 1945, 300 employees.*

Now you are ready to organize information about companies that will be of benefit to you.

Library Research Project

Instructions
Use this page for your research project. Record the information about your SIC numbers in the following space:

SIC numbers for my career area are: _____

Use some of the resources on pages 77–79 to complete this form. List data about two companies that employ people in your career field.

1. Name of local company: _____

2. Address: _____

3. Phone number: _____

4. Contact person: _____

5. Type of work: _____

6. Additional company information: _____

_____

1. Name of company not located in your area: _____

2. Address: _____

3. Phone number: _____

4. Contact person: _____

5. Type of work: _____

6. Additional company information: _____

_____

As a result of your research, ask yourself:

- How do my training, education, and personal skills meet the needs of this company?
- What is the focus of this business? Sales? Research? Manufacturing? Marketing?
- Does the salary scale meet my needs?
- What is the size of the company? Would I be comfortable here?
- Who is in charge of the area where I want to work?
- What is the projected future of this company or business?

Once you have completed the company research portion of the preinterview process, you are ready to create your cover letter. Remember, the more you know about a potential employer, the greater advantage you will have in focusing the letter on the needs of the company. This specific information will also be beneficial later during the actual interview.

WORLD OF WORK   Denise Osei, Multicultural Specialist, says: "Along with your resume it's very important to include a cover letter about your personal and technical skills, because usually an employer is looking for people with skills they don't presently have, and your resume sometimes lacks the specific information the employer needs to know about you." (*Moving into Your Future*)

3.2 GENERAL FORMAT FOR COVER LETTERS

Each time you write a cover letter, review this format for composing letters to be sure nothing is omitted or incorrect.

1. **Use appropriate paper.**
   a. Letters should be printed on $8\frac{1}{2} \times 11$ inch white paper or paper of the same color and quality as your resume. *Never* use a dot matrix printer or perforated paper.
   b. The envelope should be on paper of the same color as your resume and of standard business size, $4\frac{1}{3} \times 9\frac{1}{2}$ inches. You may want to use a larger envelope ($8\frac{1}{2} \times 12$ or 11×13) for mailing your data if you have additional information to include, such as letters of reference.
2. **Use correct main parts for a flush-left (block style, no indent) letter format.** The flush-left style simplifies formatting the letter because all of the sections align on the left margin of the paper and you do not have to tabulate across the page, as in some older styles of business correspondence.
   a. **Return address:** The heading is composed of your return address and date.
      Sample:
      204th Ave
      Racine, WI 99206
      September 12, 1997
   b. **Inside address:** Try to determine the name and the business title of the person to whom the cover letter is to be sent. An appropri-

ate business title should follow the name—"**Mr.** Rex King, **Personnel Manager,**" rather than simply "Rex King." The inside address begins four lines below the date.

Sample:

Mr. Rex King
Personnel Manger
Banhog Industries
State Street
Chicago, IL 99870

c. **Salutation:** The salutation should be "Dear Mr. King:" (not "Dear Rex,") unless you know the person very well. As in the examples of letters on pages 86, 87, 91, the proper punctuation following the salutation is a colon. The salutation begins **two lines** below the inside address.

Sample:

Mr. Rex King
Personnel Manger
Banhog Industries
State Street
Chicago, IL 99870

2 lines →

Dear Mr. King:

1 line →

If you are unable to determine who should receive the letter, use the AMS style of business letter (see the sample on page 92).

d. **Body:** The body of the letter should be single spaced, with double spacing between paragraphs. The first and last paragraphs should be kept short—about four lines. Middle paragraphs should not be over ten lines each.

e. **Complimentary closing:** "Respectfully yours" is probably too formal, but "Cordially" may be too familiar for an employment application letter. "Sincerely," followed by a comma, is usually correct. **The complimentary closing begins two lines below the last paragraph.**

f. **Signature:** One of the most common errors in writing business letters is mailing the correspondence without a signature. Write the signature in ink and print your name below it.

Sample:

Sincerely,

4 spaces →

Jerry Jones
Jerry Jones

g. **Enclosure notation:** When a resume is enclosed with the cover letter, the word "Enclosure" should be typed at the left margin, **two lines** below the typed signature line.

Sample:

Enclosure

If someone else prepares your letter, the initials of that person would follow yours.

Sample:

Enclosure
JJ/LL

3. **Use an attractive arrangement of print on the sheet of paper.**

    a. A 70-space line is probably the simplest.

    b. The return address may begin at about line 13 or line 11 for the AMS style.

    c. The flush-left format, as shown in the following letter samples, is the easiest to use.

4. Use care in proofreading.

    a. If you use a typewriter, the typewriter ribbon should be fresh and typewriter keys need to be clean to produce a sharp, legible copy.

    b. Be sure there are no misspelled words or typographical errors in the final copy and that corrections have been made neatly. When in doubt, use the dictionary or a computer spellchecker to verify the spelling.

    c. Have others proofread your material. The spellchecker on a computer will not solve all spelling problems, such as the distinction between *their* and *there*.

Your cover letter is an advance salesperson for you. You want it to work for you, so be careful when writing. You want the potential employer to have the best possible impression of you.

3.3 WRITE COVER LETTERS THAT WILL GET YOU AN INTERVIEW

Cover letters are of two distinct types, **solicited** and **unsolicited.** The solicited letter answers a newspaper advertisement or refers to a posted position. The unsolicited cover letter could be termed a **prospecting letter** because you are looking for employment "gold" with a company of interest to you. In the unsolicited letter you are trying to create interest in yourself, but you do not know if the company has any positions available in your field.

In either situation, be certain that you present yourself positively and not just as an "average" worker.

WORLD OF WORK   A job candidate from Japan believed that she needed to present herself as "average" when applying for employment. In her country, someone who puts herself above others is not respected, but to be "average" is good. The candidate then pointed out to the interviewer the Japanese proverb, "The nail that sticks out gets hit."

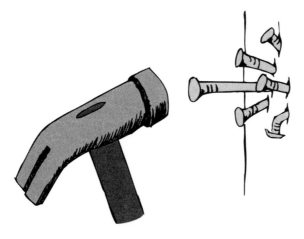

The unsolicited version of a cover letter is actually a sales letter, because you are trying to sell the company on the idea of calling you. You want them to ask you to come in for an interview even though the company may not have a job opening at this time. The fundamental steps of selling are:

1. Get attention.
2. Arouse interest.
3. Present convincing evidence.
4. Ask for action.

An unsolicited cover letter not only should follow this basic four-step formula, but also should include some references to the unique aspects of that company and the type of work they perform. Specific company information will reflect genuine interest and accurate knowledge about that company. Researching the company is a vital activity to complete prior to composing your letter.

Never have unsolicited letters mass-produced. A generic letter, without specific company information, does not demonstrate an honest desire to work for that company.

TOOLS OF COMMUNICATION

Evaluating Unsolicited Cover Letters

Instructions

With a partner or individually, review the information about Alloy Trailers on page 80. Then read the letter on page 86, which was written to them. Rate the letter using the evaluation form on page 88. How effectively does David Jessup's letter meet the four-step sales format and specific company focus? What are the strengths and weakness of the letter?

When you have finished that evaluation, rate the next unsolicited letter on page 87 according to the same standards on page 88. What are the strengths and weakness of this letter? In your opinion, which letter was more effective? Compare your scores with those of another person in class. How close were your scores? If you were in a personnel office, would you call either of these people to come in for an interview? Decide as a class how many of you would recommend interviewing none, one, or both of these applicants.

An Example of an Unsolicited Cover Letter That Could Be Sent to Alloy Trailers

West 504 Hammer Av
Newton, KS 66866
October 29, 1997

Mr. Frank Pignanelli
President
Alloy Trailers, Inc.
S. 3025 Geiger Blvd.
Spokane, WA 99204

Dear Mr. Pignanelli:

Are you interested in hiring an experienced, dependable worker with practical work experience, as well as someone having recent education in both welding and sheet metal? If so, I believe I may be the person you could be looking for.

As you can see by my enclosed resume, I also have work experience in several other technical areas. The years in the Air Force taught me how to be both a team player and a team leader with diverse groups of people.

Since I will be visiting family in the Spokane area during the Christmas holidays, I will call to see about the possibility of touring the plant and hopefully obtaining an interview with you or someone else who would be available at this time. A portfolio with photographs of my work will be available at that time. If you would like any additional information, please call me at (316) 743-5607 between 8:00 A.M. and 3:00 P.M., West Coast time.

Sincerely,

David J. Jessup

David J. Jessup

Enclosures

Another Example of an Unsolicited Cover Letter

980 Robland Avenue
Trail, British Columbia
CANADA VIR-3N1
May 20, 1998

Mr. John Clay
Trifle Equipment Limited
4532 #6 Road
Richmond, BC
CANADA V9X - 8T3

Dear Mr. Clay:

I come from an outstanding Fluid Power Technology program. I have received the best training possible the past two years at Spokane Community College, so I believe that I can be an asset to your company.

The Fluid Power Technology program includes extensive work with hydraulic systems interfaced with electrical and pneumatic control circuits, machine shop procedures and welding. In addition to the technical training in Fluid Power, I have taken courses in job communication skills, leadership development, and industrial first aid.

My work and in-class experience have given me the ability to work well with my hands, to develop manual dexterity, to work under pressure at a high level of efficiency, and to work with many types of people.

After you have had an opportunity to read my resume and the enclosed course outline, I will look forward to talking with you regarding an appointment for an interview. Please consider me for a position with your company. I will be in Vancouver during summer break, June 18–28, and could be available for an interview during those days. Also, another date could be arranged if you are not available at that time. If I have not heard from you, I will call you during the second week of July. The telephone number here at Spokane Community College is (509) 533-1111, or after 3:30 P.M., I can be reached at (509) 345-7985.

Sincerely,

Julie Smith

Julie Smith

Enclosures

<table>
<tr><td>**TOOLS OF
COMMUNICATION**</td><td>

Writing an Unsolicited Cover Letter

</td></tr>
</table>

Instructions

Write a letter to one of the two companies you researched on page 81. Use the checklist on pages 82–83 to determine if the structure is correct. The letter should not be hand-written but should be error free. This will usually require two or three revisions. When your letter is on a computer disk, it can be revised quickly. In addition, always keep a hard (printed) copy of your work, so you will have something to refer to if both your backup and regular disks are damaged or lost.

Exchange letters with another person in class and rate each other's letters using the same evaluation criteria used to evaluate Jessup's and Smith's letters. However, use a *separate* sheet of paper for your ratings, so you can each record your points in your own book on the evaluation form on this page.

Your instructor also will probably grade your letter using the same or a similar evaluation form.

Once you have an error-free letter, mail it out. Start prospecting while you are still in school. Don't stop with one company—write to two or three. But make certain *each* letter is focused on specific information pertaining to that company.

If you have developed your own web page on the Internet, be sure to include the E-mail address, along with some specific references to your individual skills and abilities.

Unsolicited Letter Evaluation Form

Factor	Possible Points	Jessup's	Smith's	Mine
1. Opening sales appeal	15			
2. Neatness, typing accuracy	15			
3. Qualifications, training, personal examples of experience	15			
4. Specific references to the work the company does	15			
5. Grammar, spelling, sentence structure, punctuation	15			
6. Where/when to reach Interview asked for	15			
7. Closing	10			
TOTAL POINTS	**100**			

3.4 SOLICITED COVER LETTERS

When writing a cover letter for an advertised position, you have an opportunity to present your case effectively. A good solicited letter will show interest, enthusiasm, knowledge of the company itself and of the position for which you are applying. You also will be demonstrating the ability to use English correctly.

Your solicited letter should contain:

1. A clearly stated **request for the position** listed in the advertisement. Include the date and place of the advertisement.
2. Your **reasons for wanting to work for the firm,** incorporating what you know about the business.
3. A brief statement about **why you think you are qualified** for this position. If you do not match *every* requirement, explain how you could adjust to meet that need or acquire added training.
4. A sentence stating that **your resume is enclosed.**
5. Information about **where and when you can be reached** for an interview.

WORLD OF WORK

Last year, while completing this project, a student discovered a company with an opening in his career. Although the job description exceeded his level of training, he E-mailed them his resume with a cover letter explaining what skills he had acquired that matched what he had learned about the company from its web pages. As a result of this communication, he received an offer for summer employment by E-mail that same day!!

The following pages contain examples of solicited cover letters. The first one has some errors. How many can you find?

Evaluating a Solicited Cover Letter

Instructions
Either individually or in small groups, see if you can identify what's wrong or missing in this letter according to the general format for letters on pages 82–83. Circle the errors, then rate it according to the evaluation form on page 93.

East 1234 10th Avenue
Spokane, WA 99306

Mrs. Joan White
Brown Products, Inc.
3329 West Main Street
Seattle, WA 98764

Dear Joan:

Perhaps you recall that I telephoned you, to inquire about the position and I was wondering why I hadn't heard from you. At that time, you invited me to send a copy of my resume which you will find enclosed in this package along with a sample of some of my recent work.

I have an Associate of Applied Science degree. My resume indicates the extent of my skills and experience. I believe that I am most qualified and could efficiently fill the position your company is seeking to staff better than any one else.

As I mentioned in our phone conversation, I am moving to the Seattle area toward the end of June and I want an interview as soon as possible. I can be reached from 8:30 a.m. to 2:30 p.m. at the college on weekdays.

I am very much looking forward to meeting with you.

Sincerely,

Jeff Brown

Jeff Brown

Enclosure

Do you recognize some of the information in the following example of a solicited letter? This is a revision of the letter you just graded on the preceding page.

An Example of a Solicited Cover Letter

East 1234 10th Avenue
Spokane, WA 99306
May 18, 1999

Mrs. Joan White
Information Center Manager
Brown Products, Inc.
3329 West Main Street
Seattle, WA 98764

Dear Mrs. White:

I am writing to you in response to your ad in the *Seattle Republic* for an entry-level programmer. Perhaps you recall that I telephoned you on Monday, June 1, to inquire about the position. At that time, you invited me to send a copy of my resume, which you will find enclosed in this package along with a sample of some of my recent work.

I have an Associate in Applied Science degree in Computer Programming. My resume indicates the extent of my skills and experience in this area. I believe that I am most qualified as an entry-level programmer and could efficiently fill the position your company is seeking to staff.

As I mentioned in our phone conversation, I am moving to the Seattle area toward the end of June. I would very much appreciate hearing from you regarding the possibility of an interview. I can be reached from 8:30 A.M. to 2:30 P.M. at the college on weekdays at (509) 533-1243. My home phone is (509) 123-4567.

If I have not heard from you by June 23, I will call to arrange for an interview when I reach Seattle. I am very much looking forward to meeting with you.

Sincerely,

Jeff Brown

Jeff Brown

Enclosure

Sometimes a position will be advertised with only a box number. In that case, you have no way of finding out the name of the person who will be reading your letter. In this situation, the Administrative Management System (AMS) style of letter can be used.

AMS Style Letter

(To be used *only* if the individual's name is unknown)

West 789 10th Avenue
Greeley, CO 99089
May 30, 1999

ABC
Personnel Department
Box 370 Greeley Tribune
Greeley, CO 99089

REQUEST FOR INTERVIEW

Recently, in the *Greeley Tribune,* I saw that you have openings for electronics technicians. I hope you will see me as the right person for the position.

For the last three years, I have been attending Weld Community College's electronics program, which emphasizes time spent at the bench. I am very eager and willing to learn a new job and to be of benefit to your company. Please refer to my enclosed resume for any information you may require.

Please notify me at (303) 987-5643 to set up an interview. I am looking forward to your call.

Mary Lake

Mary Lake

Enclosure

**TOOLS OF
COMMUNICATION**

Writing a Solicited Cover Letter

Instructions

Look in the want ads in your local newspaper, and find a position you would be qualified to fill. Research the company if the name is mentioned in the ad. Write a letter to answer the ad using the ideas on page 89 and following the format for business letters on pages 82–83. The letter should be typed and error-free. Two, three, or even more revisions are often necessary in order to develop a high-quality letter.

Exchange letters with another person in class, and rate each other's letters using the same evaluation criteria used to evaluate Brown's letter. Use a *separate* sheet of paper for your rating so you can each record your points in your own book on the evaluation form on this page.

Your instructor probably will also grade your letter using the same or a similar evaluation form.

Before you mail a cover letter, rate yourself on these factors to see if your letter gives a correct impression of your skills. It will be very helpful to ask someone familiar with this style of letter to rate it also, so you can get objective feedback about the content of your letter.

Rating Your Solicited Letter

Factor	Possible Points	Brown's Points	Lake's Points	Mine
1. Does the letter refer to a specific ad and date?	10			
2. Sales appeal of the letter	15			
3. Knowledge of the company	15			
4. Neatness and legibility	10			
5. Qualification included? Training and/or experience	15			
6. Correct grammar, spelling, sentence structure	15			
7. Does the letter ask for an interview? Does it include when and where one can be reached?	15			
8. Closing	5			
TOTAL POINTS	**100**			

3.5 CREATE INTEREST IN YOURSELF BY COMPLETING APPLICATION FORMS EFFICIENTLY

Learning how to complete an application form skillfully is an absolute necessity. If you photocopy some sample forms and practice filling them out, you will be able to take your completed, correct sample form with you to all employment interviews. This practice saves time because you can transfer information quickly from the sample form to the prospective employer's form. Some employers will dispose of an application form instead of keeping it on file if it is incomplete or messy, or if it has misspelled words.

EMPLOYER'S FILING SYSTEM FOR POORLY COMPLETED APPLICATION FORMS

WORLD OF WORK The supervisor for a machine shop said he doesn't mind if job applicants have someone else fill out the application form for them. He just doesn't want to have the form returned with the coffee stains and greasy smudges he sometimes sees. He went on to say that a messy form often indicates a disregard for quality workmanship, and his shop produces a high quality of work.

GUIDELINES FOR FILLING OUT APPLICATION FORMS

Always take a sharpened pencil, eraser, pen, and pocket dictionary with you when applying for a job. Use a copy of your completed sample application form and your resume as resources for answering questions.

1. **Read** whether you are supposed to type, print or write. If in doubt . . . print.
2. **Read** if you are to use pen or pencil. When in doubt, use a pen with black ink, not pencil or a pen with blue ink. Blue ink or pencil do not photocopy well when copies are needed.
3. **Think** before you print. Carefully read all the questions on the application, think of your complete answer, and then print your answer.
4. **Keep** the application neat and clean. Do not scribble, try to black out, or cross out mistakes. If you make a mistake, simply draw one straight line

through the mistake and write the correct word next to it or above the error. Well-done application forms should be error-free.

5. **Put** something in every appropriate block or line. If the question does not apply to you, write N/A (not applicable), a short dash (—), the word NONE, or the words DOES NOT APPLY. This shows the interviewer that you are a careful reader and have answered every question on the application blank.

6. **Know** three or four people who will say something good about you to be your references. **Ask** these people if you may use their names *before* you list them. Then ask these two questions:

   a. May I use your name as a reference?
   b. Will you give me a *good* reference?

   It is more effective to use people not already included on your resume.

   Do not use parents, relatives, or young friends, but use teachers, older friends, and former employers. Know your reference's complete name, address, phone, place of business, position in the company, and years known.

7. **Keep a record** of all information that may be necessary to fill out applications. This includes your mother's maiden name, the date of your last illness, your doctor's name and address, your medical history, starting/ending dates and addresses of your complete work history, including the supervisor's name, and your physical limitations. Take a copy of this detailed information with you whenever applying for a position.

8. **Sign** your full name. A signature consists of the following:

   a. First name   Donald J. Smithers
   b. Middle initial
   c. Family name

   When asked for your signature, **always write. Do not print.** Be sure to put your name—baptismal, given, or the name on your Social Security card. **No nicknames** like "Skippy" or "Moose."

9. **Follow all the directions** on the application form. Show the employer that you can do what he or she wants you to do right from the beginning.

10. **Spell** correctly (if you are not sure how to spell a word, try to use another word with the same meaning). That's why you need to take a pocket-sized dictionary with you!

11. **Place of birth** means the city and state where you were born, not the name of the hospital.

12. **"Job for which you are applying"** means a *specific* job title or type of work. **Do not** write "Anything." Employers expect you to state clearly what kind of work you can do.

    Incorrect: _____ Anything _____
    POSITION APPLYING FOR

    Correct: _____ Welder _____
    POSITION APPLYING FOR

13. **Remember** that the written application form is often the employer's first picture of you and a reflection of the kind of worker you are. Are you neat and detail-oriented or sloppy and careless? Show pride in yourself by filling out the application carefully. This attention to detail might at least get you an interview.

Another option for completing a job application form is to go to the personnel office ahead of time, ask for the form, photocopy it, and practice filling it out. Once you have a corrected copy of the application form, you can transfer the information to the original. **Be sure to read and follow the directions on the form.** Some employers view the inability to follow simple directions on a form as an indication of a prospective employee's inability to follow directions on the job.

TOOLS OF COMMUNICATION

Completing Application Forms Accurately

Instructions
Complete the information on the form provided for you in this book on pages 97–99. Then exchange your application form and this rating sheet with someone else in class. You may also need to exchange resumes in order to check the application for accuracy.

RATING YOUR APPLICATION FORM

Factor	Possible Points	Judged Points
1. Neatness and legibility	30	
2. Error-free	30	
3. Accuracy	40	
TOTAL POINTS	**100**	

If you are not hired or even called for an interview, many employers will keep your application on file for a period of time, along with your resume and cover letter for future reference. That is one more reason to be sure to complete your application form with the same high quality of workmanship as your resume and cover letter.

SAMPLE FORM

APPLICATION FOR EMPLOYMENT

(PLEASE PRINT PLAINLY)

THIS COMPANY PROVIDES EQUAL OPPORTUNITY IN ALL AREAS OF EMPLOYMENT AND DOES NOT DISCRIMINATE AGAINST ANY INDIVIDUAL ON THE BASIS OF RACE, COLOR, RELIGION, SEX, AGE, NATIONAL ORIGIN, MARITAL STATUS OR HANDICAP.

DATE _____

NAME _____ SOC. SEC. NO. _____
     LAST   FIRST   MIDDLE INITIAL

PRESENT ADDRESS _____
          NUMBER   STREET   CITY   STATE   ZIP

HOME PHONE NO. (____)_____ WORK PHONE NO. (____)_____
         AREA CODE   AREA CODE

DATE OF BIRTH _____ ARE YOU LEGALLY ABLE TO WORK IN THIS COUNTRY?   YES ____   NO ____
(IF UNDER 18)

POSITION OR TYPE OF EMPLOYMENT DESIRED: _____

_____ SALARY DESIRED: _____

AVAILABLE FOR: FULL TIME: ____   PART TIME: ____   TEMPORARY: ____   DATE AVAILABLE: _____

HOURS AVAILABLE: _____ DAYS AVAILABLE: _____

NAMES OF RELATIVES EMPLOYED BY THIS COMPANY: _____

INDICATE HOW YOU LEARNED OF THIS OPENING: _____

   OWN ACCORD _____   AGENCY (NAME OF AGENCY): _____

   EMPLOYEE REFERRAL (NAME OF EMPLOYEE): _____

   OTHER _____

DO YOU HAVE ANY PHYSICAL REASONS WHICH WOULD PREVENT YOU FROM PERFORMING THE SPECIFIC

KIND OF WORK FOR WHICH YOU ARE APPLYING?   YES ____   NO ____   IF YES, DESCRIBE AND EXPLAIN

THE WORK LIMITATIONS: _____

HAVE YOU EVER BEEN CONVICTED OF A FELONY? (Conviction of a crime is not an automatic bar to employment. All circumstances will be considered.)

YES _____ NO _____ IF YES, EXPLAIN: _____

MILITARY (U.S.): YES _____ NO _____ IF YES, WAS THE DISCHARGE HONORABLE? YES _____ NO _____

IF NO, PLEASE EXPLAIN THE DETAILS: _____
(Veterans may be asked to provide a copy of Discharge Form DD214)

UNDER WHAT NAME(S) WILL YOUR SCHOOL OR COLLEGE TRANSCRIPTS BE LISTED? _____

TYPE OF SCHOOL	NAME AND ADDRESS OF SCHOOL	MAJOR SUBJECT	CIRCLE LAST YR. ATTENDED	GRADUATED (GIVE DEGREE OR DIPLOMA)	LAST ATTENDED
HIGH SCHOOL			1 2 3 4		19
COLLEGE			1 2 3 4		19
GRADUATE SCHOOL			1 2 3 4		19
OTHER			1 2 3 4		19

WHAT MACHINES OR EQUIPMENT CAN YOU OPERATE? _____

BUSINESS _____

INDUSTRIAL _____

QUALIFICATION—EXPERIENCE AND/OR TRAINING _____

TYPING _____

SHORTHAND _____

DRIVER'S LICENSE? YES _____ NO _____ LICENSE NO. & STATE OF ISSUE _____ EXPIRATION DATE _____

MO   DAY   YR

SPECIAL _____

LIST BELOW ALL PRESENT AND PAST EMPLOYMENT, BEGINNING WITH YOUR MOST RECENT

1

Name and Address of Company and Type of Business	From	To	Describe the Work You Do	Weekly Starting Salary	Weekly Last Salary	Reason for Leaving	Name of Supervisor

2

Name and Address of Company and Type of Business	From	To	Describe the Work You Do	Weekly Starting Salary	Weekly Last Salary	Reason for Leaving	Name of Supervisor

3

Name and Address of Company and Type of Business	From	To	Describe the Work You Do	Weekly Starting Salary	Weekly Last Salary	Reason for Leaving	Name of Supervisor

4

Name and Address of Company and Type of Business	From	To	Describe the Work You Do	Weekly Starting Salary	Weekly Last Salary	Reason for Leaving	Name of Supervisor

May we contact the employers listed above? _____ If not, indicate by number which one(s) you

do not wish us to contact _____

PERSONAL REFERENCES (Not Former Employers or Relatives)

Name and Occupation	Address	Phone Number

PLEASE READ CAREFULLY

Read carefully the following statements and agreement before signing the application.

1. I certify that the information contained in this application is correct to the best of my knowledge and that any material misrepresentation is grounds for dismissal from the employ of _____ or rejection of my application for employment.
2. I authorize my former employers and any other persons or organizations to provide any accurate and current information they have about my background, and I release all concerned from any liability in connection therewith.
3. I agree that any future offer of employment is contingent upon my passing a physical exam(s) if required by _____.
4. I understand and agree that the first sixty (60) days of employment will be considered a probationary period.

_____   _____
DATE OF SIGNING   SIGNATURE OF APPLICANT

Affirmative Action Forms

Affirmative action forms like the one shown may be included with some application forms. It will be your choice to complete it or not.

RE: Affirmative Action

_____ has affirmative action programs for Disabled Veterans and Veterans of the Vietnam Era Veterans Readjustment Assistance Act of 1974 and the Rehabilitation Act of 1973, respectively. If you believe yourself covered by either act and wish to benefit under ("under the provisions of") the affirmative action program, please check the appropriate box below. Submission of this information is voluntary, and refusal to provide it will not subject you to discharge or disciplinary treatment. Information obtained concerning individuals shall be kept confidential, except that (1) supervisors and managers may be informed regarding restrictions on the work or duties of handicapped individuals and disabled veterans and regarding necessary accommodation; (2) first aid and safety personnel may be informed, when and to the extent appropriate, if the condition might require emergency treatment; and (3) government officials investigating compliance with the act shall be informed.

If you are handicapped or a disabled veteran, we would like to include you under the affirmative action program. It would assist us if you tell us about (1) any special methods, skills, and procedures that qualify your handicap or disability, so that accommodations that we could make would enable you to perform the job properly and safely, including special equipment, changes in the physical layout of the job, elimination of certain duties relating to the job, and other accommodations.

_____ I am a disabled veteran or veteran of the Vietnam era.

_____ I consider myself mentally or physically handicapped.

_____ I do not wish to participate in either program.

Comments:

Name _____

The _____, as an equal opportunity employer, has made a commitment to an affirmative action program and is required by state and federal guidelines, including corrective employment programs, to maintain the information. The success of our program depends on your voluntary compliance.

REMINDER: This information will be used only for the purpose of the development of statistics.

Ethnic:	_____ (1) Asian or Pacific Islander	A person having origins in any of the original peoples of the Far East, Southeast Asia, the Indian Subcontinent, or the Pacific Islands. The area includes, for example, China, Japan, Korea, the Philippine Islands, and Samoa.
	_____ (2) Black (not of Hispanic Origin)	A person having origins in any of the Black racial groups of Africa.
	_____ (3) American Indian or	A person having origins in Alaska or any of the original peoples of North America, and who maintains cultural identification through tribal affiliation or community recognition.
	_____ (4) Hispanic	A person of Mexican, Puerto Rican, Cuban, Central or South America, or other Spanish culture or origin, regardless of race.
	_____ (5) White (not of Hispanic origin)	A person having origins in any of the original peoples of Europe, North Africa, or the Middle East.

Veteran Status:	_____ (1) Veteran	
	_____ (2) Vietnam era veteran	(August 5, 1964–May 7, 1975)
	_____ (3) Disabled Vietnam veteran	Any person whose discharge from the service was for a disability incurred during the line of duty or who is entitled to a disability compensation under the laws administered by the Veterans Administration for a disability rated at 30% or more.
	_____ (4) Disabled veteran	
	Dates of service:	From: _____ to _____

Handicapped:

_____ (1) Yes

_____ (2) No

Any person who (a) has a physical or mental impairment that substantially limits one or more major life activities, (b) has a record of such impairment, or (c) is regarded as having such an impairment.

_____ (1) Male

_____ (2) Female

Date of Birth: Month _____   Day _____   Year _____

STRESS LESS   Doing paperwork such as completing job application forms and writing cover letters often creates stress in people's lives. But here is a paperwork project that can actually *reduce* stress. This stress reliever is a two-step process involving only two items—a lunch-sized paper bag and a pen or pencil.

Step 1:   On the paper bag, write down all the things that are causing stress in your life right now. What are your stressors? List factors such as:

a. Paperwork
b. Finances
c. Car
d. No job
e. Looking for a job
f. Conflict at home or school

When you have listed everything you can think of, move on to step 2.

Step 2:   Open the paper bag, gather the top quarter of the bag in one hand and blow into the bag until it is inflated. Tighten your grip on the neck of the bag. Strike the paper bag firmly with your other hand until it pops.

This stress-relieving exercise actually produces three outcomes:

a. Listing stressors can sometimes reduce stress.
b. Breathing deeply and blowing into the paper bag can restore a deep breathing pattern. Shallow breathing caused by stress creates more stress, because you have less oxygen in your body.
c. Striking the bag firmly can relieve some of the physical tension built up in your body as a result of stress.

CASE STUDY   *With a partner decide how you would resolve the following situation:*

Sarah and John have both applied for the same advertised position. According to the resumes, their training and experience are very similar. Sarah also submitted a cover letter that reflected knowledge of the company, but John's cover letter did not mention anything about the company. However, John had an application form that was neat and consistent with the information on his resume, whereas Sarah's form listed employment experience that was inconsistent with data on her resume.

If you were an employer, whom would you call for an interview? Sarah? John? Neither? Both? Explain the basis for your decision.

CHAPTER PROJECT   Working in teams, select a company in your career field, research the company, and, as a team, construct an unsolicited letter that focuses on the type of work the company specializes in producing or servicing. When the letter is completed, each team will submit it to the instructor, who will grade each team's effort. Then the class will vote on what they perceive to be the most effective letter in terms of company knowledge, sales appeal, discussion of qualifications, basic sentence structure, spelling, and punctuation.

DISCUSSION QUESTIONS

1. What are three reasons why it is important to investigate a business or company when applying for a position?
2. What are the disadvantages in using cover letters that are copied from someone else or mass produced?
3. List four elements that need to be included in an unsolicited cover letter.
4. How can you save time when filling out application forms?

SUMMARY

This chapter provided you with experience in the following:

- Researching companies for job opportunities
- Evaluating cover letters
- Writing cover letters for both unadvertised and advertised positions
- Completing application forms correctly and evaluating them

Each of these activities gives you the opportunity to create interest in yourself so that you will be called for a job interview.

CHAPTER FOUR

What Was That You Said?
Telephoning and Listening

LEARNING OBJECTIVES:

1. Understand and apply effective communication tools when using the telephone to ask about employment.

2. Learn to overcome poor listening habits by practicing active listening.

3. Learn the importance of feedback tools when listening to others.

4. Practice using direct questions and paraphrasing when communicating with others.

5. Understand barriers to successful communication, including some cultural differences.

6. Understand the communication circuit.

This chapter explains the effective use of the telephone to locate employment possibilities.

The chapter also provides opportunities to develop productive listening and feedback skills. In one communications skills survey, 140 out of 180 employers stressed the need for employees to have efficient listening skills to deal effectively with customers, co-workers, and supervisors. In fact, those employers selected listening as the number one communication skill they most desired their employees to possess (Clark).

The chapter also presents a brief discussion of communication barriers and cultural differences to make you aware of why some communication problems occur. It closes with an overview of the communication circuit to emphasize the role of listening in the communication process.

4.1 USING THE TELEPHONE DURING EMPLOYMENT SEARCHES

When making a telephone call to inquire about a job opening or to request an interview, avoid calling during the first hour of business on a Monday or on Friday or Saturday afternoon. On Monday, most businesses are trying to get work organized, and on the last day of the work week, extra time is often needed to complete projects. Your phone call could be an unwelcome interruption unless the position you are calling about has just been advertised. In that situation, the employer may want a quick response.

Every time you use the telephone, you are actually projecting your presence into somebody's home or office. Your voice should create a favorable impression. Observe the following telephone courtesies:

- **Before placing a call, have your thoughts well organized.** Then you will be able to proceed in a direct, orderly manner. Write down all your ideas in advance so you will not forget something important. Have necessary reference materials right by the phone, such as information about the position and the company. Your resume and work history should also be available.
- **Let the phone ring seven to ten times before you hang up.** The person you are calling may be busy and unable to answer your call in three or four rings.
- **Drop your voice into warm, friendly tones.** Concentrate on establishing vocal contact to compensate for the lack of visual contact.
- **Call only when necessary, and be brief when you do call.** In business, time means money. Do not call about employment so often that you would be considered an annoyance.
- **When leaving a message on someone's voice mail or answering machine, speak slowly, distinctly, and directly into the phone.** This is especially important when leaving telephone numbers or any other message involving numbers. Give the date and time of your call. Identify yourself by stating your full name (not just your first name; the person replaying your call later may know several people with the same name). It is always a good idea to repeat your name and telephone number again just before hanging up.

How to Be Understood Clearly on the Telephone

Sounds, words, and numbers can be difficult to interpret on the phone. You can use some of these ideas to eliminate confusion:

When you are spelling your name or the correct spelling of names and addresses is important, this code helps in differentiating between often-confused letters such as B and D, F and S, or B and V. You can verify letters by using the method commercial and military pilots often practice.*

A	*Alpha*	*H*	*Hotel*	*O*	*Oscar*	*V*	*Victor*
B	*Beta*	*I*	*India*	*P*	*Papa*	*W*	*Whiskey*
C	*Charlie*	*J*	*Juliet*	*Q*	*Quebec*	*X*	*X-ray*
D	*Delta*	*K*	*Kilo*	*R*	*Romeo*	*Y*	*Yankee*
E	*Echo*	*L*	*Lima*	*S*	*Sierra*	*Z*	*Zulu*
F	*Foxtrot*	*M*	*Metro*	*T*	*Tango*		
G	*Golf*	*N*	*Nectar*	*U*	*Uniform*		

If you are not understood when you are spelling your name, try using this verification list. The list can also be helpful as you listen to others and want to be sure you have the correct spelling of names or words.

A variation of the method is used in this example. The name Brad Fischer could be clarified this way:

My name is Brad Fischer—"B" as in "Beta," "R" as in "Romeo," "A," "D" as in "Delta" [pause] "F" as in "Foxtrot," "I," "S" as in "Sierra," "C" as in "Charlie," "H," "E," "R" as in Romeo.

When repeating numbers to a caller, the proper articulation for the phone number 415-334-2514, is: "area code four one five (pause) three, three four (pause) two five (pause) one four."

The phone number 702-769-2500 is pronounced: "area code seven zero two (pause) seven six nine (pause) two five zero zero."

When making an appointment for an interview for an advertised position:

1. Identify yourself.
2. Ask if this is a convenient time to call. If not, ask, "When may I call back?"
3. Ask if the position is still open. If so, state your information briefly.
4. If you need to mail your resume, ask for the name of the person who should receive it, as well as your cover letter.
5. If there is no opening, determine whether or not they accept resumes to keep on file. If they do, mail yours to them.
6. Thank the person you spoke with, regardless of the response.

---

*Used by permission, Richard D. Clark, USAF pilot, retired.

Telephone calls for employment information could develop like one of these three situations.

Situation A: Is there still a job opening?

1. Hello, my name is Tom Maxwell and I called about your advertisement for an electronics technician. Is this a convenient time for me to call?

If the answer is no, go to situation B.
   If the answer is yes, then proceed:

2. Is the position still open?

If this answer is also yes, ask:

3. Are you making appointments for job interviews, or do you want me to mail my resume and cover letter?

If you get a yes to the first part of that question, that is great, but it does not happen very often. If the person you are talking to wants you to send your cover letter and resume first, ask:

4. To whom should the letter be addressed? What is his or her position?

If you are unable to find a specific name, ask if there is a department where your information should be directed. It will be helpful to ask one more question:

5. May I please pick up an application form ahead of time?

If this is possible, you can have the time to fill it out carefully to avoid making mistakes. When this is not allowed, take the sample form from Chapter Three with you for reference.
   At any rate, close the call by saying:

6. Thank you for your time, Mr./Ms. _____.

Always try to use the person's name during your conversation, because it makes the call more personal and less sterile.

Situation B: Can't talk now.

If this time is not convenient, ask:

> When would be a better time for me to call?

If you are told to call back later, don't assume you know what someone else means by "later." Does "later" mean "later today"? Tomorrow? In a week? Be sure to clarify, ask:

> Do you mean later today?

If the answer is yes, verify the time.

> What time?
> *or*
> Before or after 3:00 P.M.?

When calling from a different time zone, ask if your return call is to be made according to their time zone:

> Do you mean East Coast time or Mountain Standard time?

Verify the time by repeating what you understand:

> All right, I'll look forward to talking to you today between 3:00 and 4:00 P.M. Thank you for your time.

Situation C: No opening!

If someone has already been hired, ask:

> If I send you my resume, will you keep it on file? For how long?

This is a good question for two reasons:

1. Many companies call people whose resumes are kept in their files before advertising the position.
2. Perhaps the person they just hired will not work out, and you might be considered for the job if your resume and cover letter are available.

If this company does not keep resumes on file, ask if the company will be hiring soon or if they know of another company needing someone with your skills. Close with a sincere expression of your appreciation for their time.

TOOLS OF COMMUNICATION

Telephoning

Instructions

Use an audio tape recorder/player and work in a three-person team. Use this outline to make an appointment for an employment interview, with one person as the caller:

1. Identify yourself.

2. Ask if it is a good time to call; if not, determine when it would be convenient.

3. Ask if the position is open.

4. If the position is available,

   - Ask who makes appointments for interviews or if you should first send a cover letter and resume.

   - Ask if the position has been filled, whether they keep resumes on file.

   - Thank the person.

The second person represents the company and uses each of these responses:

1. Yes, there is a job opening

2. This is not a convenient time for a telephone call

3. The position has been filled

The third team member serves as the observer, who operates the recorder and provides feedback on the audio rating scale on p. 110.

Rotate positions until each team member has a chance to practice asking questions, answering them, and observing. Then all of the callers should listen to themselves and evaluate their telephone techniques using the same rating scale they received from their observer. Finally, as a group, discuss effective and ineffective answers, tone of voice, rate of speech, enthusiasm, and so on.

If you are doing this alone:

   - Practice out loud.

   - Use an audio tape recorder/player to see how you sound.

   - Play it back and listen to yourself, and evaluate yourself on the audio rating scale. Ask another person out of class to listen to the tape to evaluate you using the audio rating scale and to give you ideas about how you sound.

   - Do you sound pleasant? Energetic? Enthusiastic?

   - Is your voice loud enough?

ANSWERING INTERVIEW QUESTIONS

Interviewee _____

Your name _____

	Fair 3	Good 4	Excellent 5
Wording the answer			
Use complete sentences			
Positive answer			
Was specific			
Voice			
Volume			
Interest and enthusiasm			
Sounded positive			
Energy level			
Total			

Comments

ANSWERING INTERVIEW QUESTIONS

Interviewee _____

Your name _____

	Fair 3	Good 4	Excellent 5
Wording the answer			
Use complete sentences			
Positive answer			
Was specific			
Voice			
Volume			
Interest and enthusiasm			
Sounded positive			
Energy level			
Total			

Comments

4.2 IS POOR LISTENING A PROBLEM?

How many times have you heard yourself say, "I'm sorry, what did you just say?" or "Would you please repeat that?"

What is the problem? Why do we have difficulty concentrating on what others tell us even when it could mean money in our pockets—like getting a job or a raise?

One aspect of the problem is that people often think of communication as *talking* or writing. Yet, according to one of the pioneers in the study and research of listening, Dr. Ralph Nichols:

> *45% of our awake time is spent listening*
> *30% of it is spent speaking*
> *16% of it is reading*
> *9% of our awake time is spent writing.*
> (*Jones, pp. 17, 18*)

Nichols found that without training we listen with a shocking

25% efficiency!

He also reported that out of any ten-minute briefing, the untrained listener will lose 75 percent of what was said after two hours.

One of the primary causes of listening inefficiency is our "thought speed." Most people can think at a speed of 500 to 800 words per minute, but many speakers talk about 125 words per minute. Consequently, a listener is mentally going someplace about four times faster than a speaker, teacher, supervisor, or customer ("He Who Has Ears" lecture).

Research conducted by Lyman K. Steil, special listening consultant for the Sperry Corporation, emphasized the cost of poor listening:

> *With more than 100 million workers in America, a simple ten dollar listening mistake by each of them would cost a billion dollars. Letters have to be retyped; appointments rescheduled; shipments reshipped. And when people in large corporations fail to listen to one another, the results are even costlier. Ideas get distorted by as*

much as 80% *as they travel through the chain of command. Employees feel more and more distant, and ultimately alienated, from top management.*

He went on to report these alarming statistics concerning the flow of information in business:

When the message originates with the **chairman of the board:**

- 67% of the message gets to the **vice-president.**
- 56% of that message from vice-president goes to the **general supervisor.**
- 40% of the same information from general supervisor is passed on to the **plant manager.**
- 30% of the message from plant manager moves on to the **foreman.**

  BUT
  ONLY

- **20% of that original message is received by the workers on the line!**

(*Sperry Listening Workbook,* 73)

As a result of these findings, some large corporations are spending much money to open communication from the bottom to the top in management by teaching their employees at all levels how to listen more productively.

WORLD OF WORK   This statement in the fluid-power publication *Compressed Air Magazine* underscores the idea that listening should move in the opposite direction—from the bottom to the top.

> Ideally, communication goes upwards, not downwards. It does not begin with managers telling their employees what's what. It begins with the subordinate's interest, then works its way up to the manager, so that the manager will then have something to communicate that is intelligible and palatable to the subordinate. Peter Drucker believes that "Nothing connected with understanding, let alone with motivation, can be communicated downward." (p. 21)

The worst listening habits, according to Dr. Nichols, are:

1. Calling a subject uninteresting or boring
2. Getting overstimulated and judging the message before the speaker finishes speaking
3. Listening for facts only
4. Faking attention
5. Tolerating outside noises or interferences that hinder listening accuracy
6. Avoiding listening to difficult material
7. Letting emotional words used by the speaker develop mental interference, inhibiting our ability to listen rationally
8. Wasting the time differential between speaking and listening. Remember, 125–150 words per minute is the rate of conversational speech, while 500–800 words per minute is your thinking speed

("He Who Has Ears" lecture)

4.3 OVERCOMING POOR LISTENING HABITS

You can become a better listener by:

1. **Focusing your five senses on the speaker's message.**
   Realize listening is work! Sit up, feel alive, look the speaker in the eye. Listen with concentrated attention to overcome outside distractions. Do not fake attention.

2. **Making sure you have the correct understanding about what the speaker wants to convey.** Listen to detect central ideas, not just facts. Ask questions, paraphrase, and check your perception. Learn to control your emotions as you listen. This is the hardest part, but simple awareness will take you a long way toward becoming a better listener. Once you have the correct understanding, you can decide on your opinion and respond accordingly.

   Once you make the decision to *really* listen, there are specific procedures you can use to increase your listening efficiency. Listed here are some methods for improving your listening skills.

The Ten Best Listening Habits

1. Tune in to see what will be of interest to you, even if you think you have heard it all before.
2. Get the meaning of the message, which is much more important than the speaker's appearance, mannerisms, or poor grammar—do not let these things distract you.
3. Hear everything the speaker has to say before you judge him or her.
4. Listen for a brief time before taking notes to determine the critical elements of the message.

5. Listen for main ideas, principles, and concepts, as well as facts.
6. Listen with energy. Relaxing while listening is *not* helpful. In good listening, there is a collection of energy and tension inside of you. When you are receiving directions or during a job interview, is no time to sit and nod your head vaguely while your mind is elsewhere.
7. Get up and do something about distractions—shut a window, close a door, ask the speaker to speak louder, or ask the person next to you to be quiet so you can concentrate on what the speaker is saying.
8. Learn to listen to difficult material or different points of view on television and radio to practice the skill of listening objectively.
9. Identify your own greatest verbal and nonverbal barriers. Is it a person's frown or someone calling you "stupid" that causes you to stop listening?
10. Make thought speed an asset instead of a liability by mentally summarizing and analyzing what has already been said rather than daydreaming about your plans for the weekend or planning what you will say next.

Adapted from Ralph Nichols, "10 Keys to Good Listening," quoted in Jones, pp. 16, 17.

TOOLS OF COMMUNICATION

Practicing Effective Listening Techniques

Instructions
Circle three of the preceding ten good listening habits you need to develop, and list them below. Use the listening log to check and improve your listening skills during the next week. Bring your log to class. In small groups, record which habits are in greatest need of further development. Do a class tally to determine the most common listening weaknesses. Since all good habits are established through repetition, repeat the exercise for another week.

1. _____

2. _____

3. _____

WORLD OF WORK

"During a job interview, listening well is even more important than answering questions well," points out Sharna Fey, a regional recruiter for the Marriott Corporation.

1. Write down one on-the-job or school situation in the past where a misunderstanding occurred.
   a. What was the listening problem in that situation?

   b. What could you have said or done to avoid this problem? Write down your preferred wording or action.

2. During the next week, write down three examples of situations where you need to listen carefully. How did you respond? Which good listening techniques did you use? Which ones did you forget?
   a. First listening situation

   Your response:

   _____

   b. Second listening situation

   Your response:

   _____

   c. Third listening situation

   Your response:

   _____

3. Now analyze your listening. Do you have trouble following instructions? Why or why not? Do you overreact emotionally? Do distractions interrupt your listening?

   _____

4. Which *listening* behaviors can you adopt from pages 113–114 to improve your relationships both at work and in your personal life? Refer again to the Ten Best Listening Techniques on pages 113–114; select at least two more to practice for one more week while you listen to those around you.

_____

Continue trying these ideas with friends and co-workers over the next few weeks. If you do this consistently, you will undoubtedly see noticeable changes in how others react to you. It has been said that a habit must be repeated **21 times** to become an integrated skill, so keep working to incorporate efficient listening skills as another tool in your personal communication toolbox.

The careful analysis of your listening skills can assist you in becoming a more effective, active listener, not only on the job but also in your social life and at home.

There are characteristics you can develop in order to become a more effective active listener. Active listeners can be described as:

1. Being open-minded about people who look or sound different from themselves
2. Able to follow several methods of organization—even poorly organized material can be listened to with some degree of tolerance
3. Able to hear conclusions, inferences, generalizations, and the like, along with the facts
4. Likely to listen even more attentively when the material becomes difficult, because they see it as a challenge to them
5. Able to use paraphrasing to clarify their understanding of what someone has said

One conclusion we can draw from these statements is that active listening is not an easy skill to acquire. It demands energetic involvement and interaction with others. Research has shown that heart rate, pulse, and blood pressure increase when you are truly involved in the listening process (as seen in the film *Power of Listening*).

Part of the acquisition of effective listening procedures can be accomplished by using communication feedback tools.

4.4 PARAPHRASING: A COMMUNICATION FEEDBACK TOOL

One critical feedback tool to use when telephoning, interviewing for a job, or later when relating to others on the job is the skill called **paraphrasing.**

What Is Paraphrasing?

Any time we put together a message to communicate with someone, the words we use create an image in the mind of the other person. We cannot always be sure that our message will have the same meaning to others as it has for us. Most people tend to assume what they understand from a statement is what the speaker intended. Paraphrasing is one way to check to be sure you understood the speaker's message. When you paraphrase **you are not giving advice or making judgments.** Paraphrasing is a way of saying to another person, "This is what **your** words mean to me."

Paraphrasing is:

1. Letting the other person know **what you understand** his or her words to mean by checking out the specific meaning.
2. Letting others know you care and are interested in what they are saying.

There are two types of paraphrases. Paraphrasing for **content** (facts) means letting the other person know what you understood his or her meaning of ideas and thoughts to be. Paraphrasing for **intent** (feelings) means checking on your understanding of the emotions you think you hear being communicated. Here is an example of each type of paraphrasing:

Paraphrasing for Content (Facts)

> **Interviewer:** I'll meet you at the door after lunch.
>
> **You:** (*paraphrasing*) Do you mean inside of the door to the building at 1:00?
>
> **Interviewer:** No! I meant outside of the door to the shop at 12:30. We take a lunch break at 11:30.

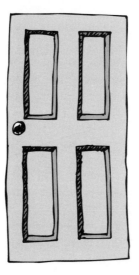 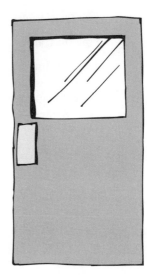

You can see the importance of clarifying meaning. Otherwise you could end up in the wrong place at the wrong time. Don't assume you know what the other person means. Verify!

Paraphrasing for Intent (Feelings)

> **Janice:** It's 10:30.
>
> **Neal:** You sound really discouraged. What's wrong?
>
> **Janice:** I am. I've worked two hours, and I still can't seem to get this job done right! Have any ideas?

Why Do You Paraphrase?

Paraphrasing increases the accuracy of communication. It provides feedback by revealing what the other person's statements mean to you. Paraphrasing gives you an opportunity to show them you care and are trying to listen and understand what is being said. Paraphrasing can be a valuable way to avoid or reduce conflict because you are lessening the opportunity for misunderstanding by clarifying meanings.

When Do You Paraphrase?

Obviously, we cannot paraphrase everything others say, but there are times when it is especially important to use this skill. Some of these situations are:

1. When the message is long or complicated
2. If the message seems unclear and could have more than one meaning
3. Any time you are receiving instructions
4. If you are having a negative emotional response to something someone has said

How Do You Paraphrase?

To paraphrase, you simply state in your own words what the other person's message means to you. If John says: "I'm having a terrible quarter" you realize that "terrible quarter" could have many meanings.

To paraphrase, tell John what you think he meant. You might say,

"You mean you are taking too many classes?"

At this point, John can agree, or can tell you what he really meant to say. It is not necessary for your paraphrase always to take the form of a question. You could paraphrase the same message by simply responding with a statement, such as: "I know what you mean, it's a pain to take too many classes" (Roach, unpublished exercise).

Paraphrases often start with phrases such as, "You mean . . ." or "To you this means . . ." or "You're saying . . . ," However, you can word it in any way that is comfortable for you. The purpose of the question is to tell the other person what his or her message means to you.

You may wonder why not just ask a simple direct question such as "Why?" or "What's wrong?" *Who, what, where, why* questions are still appropriate to use, but they can cause some people to feel under attack, and you may not get the detailed information you need. Remember when you were a teenager and a conversation like this took place?

> **Parent:** Where did you go?
>
> **You:** Out.
>
> **Parent:** What did you do?
>
> **You:** Nothing.

Or perhaps a conversation with a supervisor sounded like this:

> **Office manager:** This job isn't done right.
>
> **You:** What's wrong?
>
> **Office manager:** You figure it out.

This last conversation would be more productive with a paraphrase, because you will get detailed information more quickly about "What *is* wrong."

> **Office manager:** This job isn't done right.
>
> **You:** Is it the color or the size that's wrong?
>
> **Office manager:** It's the color.

Specific paraphrasing helps you make corrections rapidly without wasting time guessing.

Direct Questions and Paraphrasing

Direct questions usually include *who, what, when, where, why,* and *how* words. These questions can be useful when you need information from someone who is giving you instructions.
   Here are examples of direct questions following instructions:

> **General contractor:** Bring me the blueprints.
>
> **Carpenter:** Where are they?
>
> **General:** On the shelf.
>
> **Carpenter:** What shelf?
>
> **General:** The shelf by the door.
>
> **Carpenter:** What door?
>
> **General:** I'm in a hurry, just go look for them.

Paraphrasing questions can be used to gain information quickly and are a way to narrow the options in order to get specific information more rapidly than direct questions. This particular communication tool is one way to find the detailed information you need without sounding like a lawyer conducting an interrogation.
   Here is an example of paraphrasing questions following the same instructions:

> **General contractor:** Bring me the blueprints.
>
> **Carpenter:** Are they in the pickup?
>
> **General:** No, they are on the shelf.
>
> **Carpenter:** The shelf by the kitchen door?
>
> **General:** No, the one in the bedroom.

Learning to use the paraphrasing tool takes effort and practice until you become comfortable, but the results are worth the time spent because your understanding of the meanings of other people's words will be improved.

Getting Information, Part 1

Instructions
Now try the next two situations with a partner using *both* tools—**direct questions** and **paraphrasing.** Share your results with the class.

1. Supervisor: Get a different part for this machine.

   You: (direct question)

   You: (paraphrasing)

2. Supervisor: I need you to work late today.

   You: (direct question)

   You: (paraphrasing)

Paraphrasing, Part 2

Instructions
Complete numbers 1, 2, and 3 in class with a partner. Then compare your answers with the class. Several different interpretations can be correct.
   Paraphrase the following for **content—facts.**

1. Customer: This equipment isn't running right!

   Service rep:

   Customer:

2. Instructor: Your diagram is inaccurate. I'd like you to do it over.

   Student:

   Instructor:

Paraphrase the following for **intent—checking the feeling of the speaker.**

3. Bruce: This job just doesn't seem to be for me!

   Barbara:

   Bruce:

   Barbara:

   Bruce:

Paraphrasing, Part 3

Instructions

Paraphrase the following situations out of class, and bring your efforts to class for the instructor to check.

Paraphrase for Content (facts)

4. Helen: [*downcast expression in eyes and face*] I'd looked forward to my vacation, but now I don't know what to do.

You:

Helen:

Paraphrase for Intent (Feelings)

5. Customer: Would you believe it! [*His eyes are shooting sparks, his face is flushed and he's slightly out of breath.*] It took me twenty minutes to find a parking spot!

You:

Customer:

6. Write a short conversation of your own, dealing with paraphrasing for *both* content and intent. Indicate which is which.

Paraphrasing Specific Careers, Part 4

Instructions

The next exercise involves the use of paraphrasing for electrical maintenance technicians. However, it can be adapted for use in other careers, using the terminology for that field.

Name _____

Industrial Electricity/Electrical Maintenance example:

Supervisor: I want a transformer bank tied so that I have 208/120 volts.

Employer: O.K., you want that transformer tied on a delta connection.

Supervisor: No, in a Y connection, O.K.?

Directions: Please complete the following by paraphrasing for content.

1. Jim: I want you to put a service in.

Bill: _____

Jim: _____

2. Instructor: Your schematic is inaccurate, Alex. I'd like you to do it over.

Alex: _____

Instructor: _____

3. Steve: I would like to have you look at the main turbine motor.

Ed:_____

Steve: _____

4. Bob: John should never have gone into the field.

Don: _____

Bob: _____

5. Judy: I would like you to hook up a boiler feedpump.

Mike:_____

Judy: _____

(Roach, unpublished exercise)

4.5 COMMUNICATION BARRIERS

Barriers to communication sometimes interrupt the successful completion of the communication process, causing an interruption in the flow of information. What are some of those barriers?

Barrier 1. Language: Words with multiple meanings often cause great confusion in the mind of the person receiving the message. Just think how many different definitions exist for the simple word *bar*—candy bar, salad bar, legal bar, ballet bar, metal bar! How many different meanings for *rock* can you think of? Many words are vague and cause confusion. What about a supervisor who orders you to "get this work done soon"? Does he or she mean within minutes, an hour, or sometime this week?

Barrier 2. Social: Thinking someone is above or beneath your social status can hinder honest communication. You may communicate quite differently with a co-worker on the line than you would with a supervisor in the office.

Barrier 3. Emotional: Being angry, upset, or even looking forward to payday can cause a person to be distracted, thus stopping the flow of communication.

Barrier 4. Physical: Distracting noises or a personal hearing loss may contribute to an increase of static on the communication hotline.

Barrier 5. Listening: Most people listen at a shockingly low 25 percent rate of efficiency (see page 111). Improving listening and feedback skills is crucial to **getting the job** and **being successful on the job.**

Barrier 6. Cultural Differences: In today's global economy, cultural understanding is essential for a communication environment without barriers. We tend to judge others by our own standards, so we sometimes think people who are different are "weird" or wrong. Remember, **different** does not mean **deficient.** Diversity can bring an added positive point of view to the workplace. Since different cultures may have different values when relating to others at work, it will be helpful to have a general understanding of some of these differences.

Culture A has beliefs and values quite different from those of Culture B. Put an X by the number that best describes the cultural values with which you most closely identify?

Cultural Comparisons

Culture A			*Culture B*
1	2	3	4
Task oriented Let's get the job done. Work comes first, before family.			*People oriented* Concerned about the needs of workers, but family priorities come first.
1	2	3	4
Linear thinking and working Uses an orderly sequence of events. Finishes one step before going on to the next.			*Nonlinear thinking and working* Typically works on and thinks about several projects at one time (e.g., being on the phone with a customer while filling out a request for department supplies at the same time)
1	2	3	4
Direct conflict confrontation A "get the cards on the table" or "What's wrong here?" attitude: "Let's talk about our problems."			*Avoidance of direct conflict* Peace and harmony must be maintained at all costs. Face-saving techniques such as indirect suggestions are used. This approach to problem solving says, "Perhaps a person could try this method." Conflict is avoided at all costs.
1	2	3	4
Informal, casual communication styles Call the boss by his or her first name. Willing to discuss most of what's going on in life with almost anyone. "Everybody's a buddy."			*Formal ways of speaking to others* Supervisors, older people, and even co-workers are spoken to formally ("Mr.," "Miss") until they are known well. Personal problems are not discussed at work. Few friendships are formed, and these are created slowly.
1	2	3	4
Preference for working alone *Family* includes only parents and children. Friendships are often of short duration.			*Preference for working in groups* *Family* includes aunts, uncles, cousins. Close friends are viewed as brothers and sisters, and friendships are for a lifetime.

An awareness of some of our own communication barriers along with even a small degree of knowledge of cultural differences can assist you in the successful completion of communication transactions.

Is understanding people from other countries good for business?

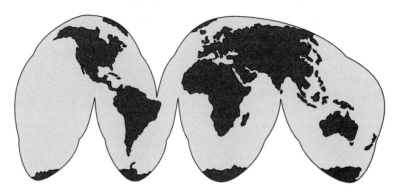

There will be more about working with some cultural differences in subsequent chapters.

4.6 COMMUNICATION RULES

Communication rules also affect the communication circuit. We are usually taught these rules as children and often take them with us into our adult life. What were your early childhood communication rules? One rule around my own house was, "Don't interrupt anyone in authority." Another was "Don't yell at people, even if you're angry." On the other hand, in a large family the communication rule might be that *only* the *loudest* voice gets heard. You can imagine the problems that occur when someone from a "Be Quiet" family and an "Only Loudness Wins" person work together on a team! Violations of personal communication rules can take place in the shop, office, or boardroom, causing a breakdown in the communication process.

4.7 WHAT IS THE COMMUNICATION CIRCUIT?

Many people would define communication as writing, talking, or waiting to talk. However, there are two indispensable components of the communication circuit—**listening efficiently** and **producing accurate feedback.** Just as electricity cannot be delivered over a circuit if the connection is incomplete, neither can a spoken message be delivered if there are barriers to the completion of the communication circuit. These communication barriers can take the form of either nonlistening and/or lack of feedback.

The communication circuit can be diagrammed to look like this model.

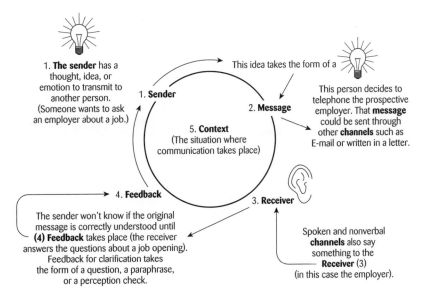

1. **The sender** has a thought, idea, or emotion to transmit to another person. (Someone wants to ask an employer about a job.)

1. **Sender**

5. **Context** (The situation where communication takes place)

This idea takes the form of a

2. **Message**

This person decides to telephone the prospective employer. That **message** could be sent through other **channels** such as E-mail or written in a letter.

4. **Feedback**

The sender won't know if the original message is correctly understood until **(4) Feedback** takes place (the receiver answers the questions about a job opening). Feedback for clarification takes the form of a question, a paraphrase, or a perception check.

3. **Receiver**

Spoken and nonverbal **channels** also say something to the **Receiver** (3) (in this case the employer).

Understanding the complexity of the communication circuit can assist you in knowing how breakdowns occur. Once a breakdown is identified it can be avoided or at least repaired. Communication breakdowns are often called "noise" or "static" since they interfere with an accurate understanding of a message. The causes of this noise are those six barriers to communication discussed previously:

- Language
- Social
- Emotional
- Physical
- Listening
- Cultural

Breakdowns in communication can happen at any point in a conversation.

WORLD OF WORK   **A "Noisy" Job Interview**

Problem noises during a job interview develop while Joe is being interviewed by Sarah. He begins to talk negatively (his *message*) about the Barnes Company, his previous employer, and he uses poor eye contact (the *channel*). These two events cause Sarah (the *receiver*), who is interviewing him, to quit listening to him. She starts thinking about Joe's negative words and lack of eye contact.

Because of Sarah's nonlistening, she doesn't hear what he said later. Joe went on to stress how he changed his original negative attitude toward the Barnes company to a positive one. He also said he left there with excellent references, but Sarah heard none of this because she was not listening.

Because of her poor listening habits, she made a snap judgment about Joe, classifying him as a negative person. She failed to ask any questions (get feedback) because she had decided *not* to hire him while she was *not* listening to what else he said.

A diagram of this dysfunctional communication circuit would look like this:

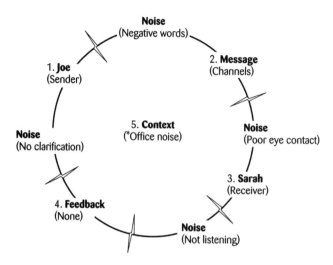

*Joe is uncomfortable in an office setting because he had expected the interview to take place in the shop. In addition, he has never been interviewed by a woman. He found it very hard to concentrate in this situation, which probably accounted for his poor eye contact.

Because of the "noisy" communication circuit, Joe and Sarah both lost. Joe lost out on an employment opportunity because of his poor eye contact and ineffective choice of words. Sarah lost a potentially productive employee because of her inefficient listening skills and lack of feedback.

Inadequate communication, talking too much, or being misunderstood can create stress in our lives. Another way to relieve stress is to analyze what we put into our bodies.

STRESS LESS ## Get Healthy by Eating Healthful Foods

Relaxing is one way to reduce stress. Another method is to become more physically fit. Ideas for doing this were included in earlier chapters. Reducing the intake of caffeine, salt, nicotine, alcohol, and sugar can also reduce stress levels. A person can further reduce stress by:

- Eating foods that are low in fat and high in fiber
- Reducing consumption of foods like coffee, cola drinks, chocolate, tea, candy, and ice cream
- Consuming more foods with a high fiber content, such as whole wheat products, broccoli, cauliflower, potatoes (with low-fat toppings), spinach, and lettuce (suggestions adapted from Deaconess Medical Center Cardiac Rehabilitation Center)

CASE STUDY *As team leader, you talked to a co-worker about her poor work production. You told her that her attitude was good but her performance was weak and she needed to improve her production level. Later she told another team member that she got a really good performance evaluation. She went on to say she does not need to change the way she does her work because you gave her a very positive performance evaluation. In the process of listening to you, she filtered out anything negative you said to her. Her selective listening attitude is reported to you. In work teams, decide how you would handle this poor listening situation.*

CHAPTER PROJECT In teams of three to five people, develop a paraphrasing exercise focused on your area of training. When your team has completed the situation specific to your work setting, exchange your exercise with another team and complete your team's responses to their project. Share the results with the class.

DISCUSSION QUESTIONS

1. What problems have you encountered when telephoning businesses for any reason?
2. Which poor listening habits are the most annoying to you?
3. Which of the feedback skills do you prefer using, direct questions or paraphrasing questions? Why?
4. Which of the barriers to communication do you believe create the greatest problems when doing business?

SUMMARY

This chapter provided you with opportunities to learn and practice:

- Effective employment searches using the telephone
- Efficient listening skills
- Productive feedback tools
- Understanding barriers to communication and cultural differences
- Understanding the communication circuit

Using these skills on a consistent basis will help you to improve customer relations, communication at work, and communication in personal relationships.

CHAPTER FIVE

The Interview: Preparing Well and Doing Your Best

LEARNING OBJECTIVES

1. Understand what employers look for during an interview.

2. Understand the preinterview process as well as interviewing do's and don't's.

3. Become familiar with the structure of interviews.

4. Practice answering typical interview questions.

5. Practice asking productive questions of the interviewer.

6. Practice participating in screening interviews and learn to evaluate them.

7. Know the importance of thank you letters, and practice writing one to the interviewer(s).

The lack of adequate planning for an interview is the greatest single fault in the interviewing process. Even if your resume and letter of application are effective enough to get you an interview, you can't sit back and take the attitude, "I've got it made." You need to know how to communicate your personal skills, abilities, and work history effectively during the interview.

The survey in Chapter One reported the communication skills applicants need to possess when interviewing for a job. Opportunities to practice these skills will be provided in this chapter.

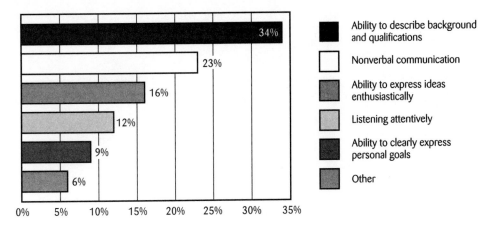

The communication skills that most affect the outcome of the interview

WORLD OF WORK   ## What Else Does It Take?

What else do employers like to hear about during a job interview? During a televised employment seminar, a panel of employers stressed which qualities they look for in job candidates:

John Dacquistas, engineer, stressed the need for potential employees to differentiate themselves from the norm. He said he prefers the presentation of portfolios rather than resumes during job interviews because interviewers can get a better picture of the type of work a potential employee is able to produce. He went on to say that he has hired people because of the quality of their portfolio.

Molly Preston of Pathology Associates said, "I receive about 100 resumes per week, and 25 percent are screened out, never to be called, because of spelling errors."

Ivan Bush, School District 81, appreciates those who show flexibility, believe in themselves, value diversity, and have done some type of volunteer work in the community.

("Employment Seminar")

Different employers often seek different attributes in a potential employee. However, all employers stressed the need to know yourself, to know your goals, and to be able to share that information with enthusiasm during the interview.

This chapter will explain the preinterview and interview processes, help you express yourself clearly and positively to a potential employer, and show you how to follow up the interview effectively.

5.1 PREPARING FOR THE INTERVIEW: REVIEW YOUR SELF-ANALYSIS

The employment interview is an arranged conversation between two or more people. It is a time to exchange conversation, an opportunity to let the interviewer know why you are the best person for the job. Being successful in the employment interview takes time, effort, planning, and good time management. Be sure to review the attitude and interest analysis you completed in Chapter One in order to talk about yourself in an organized manner. Review the techniques for researching a company that were presented in Chapter Three, so you will ask appropriate questions of the interviewer. Now, let's focus on what occurs during productive interview preparation.

Before you move through the door of the interviewer's office or shop, you should:

- Know yourself and be able to talk about your:
  Strengths/weaknesses
  Employment background, including all the places you have worked
  Education and specialized training.
  Short- and long-range goals
- Know what you want from the job:
  The type of work environment you prefer
  Whether you would rather work alone or as part of a group
  Your salary needs
  Whether you are willing to move if you get the job
- Know the company by:
  Finding out what the company produces or what service they provide
  Walking through the offices or shops if possible, and being prepared to show interest by asking questions
  Trying to talk to some employees. Don't disrupt the flow of work. If the information you discovered is positive, quote the employees during the interview.
- Know the description of the position you are interviewing for:
  What is the experience level needed for the position?
  What training will you need to complete if you get the job?
  How do you match the job description?

TOOLS OF COMMUNICATION

Interview Checklist

Use this checklist *every time* you prepare for an interview, no matter how many times you were interviewed in the past. Information about your goals or about the company may have changed since the last time you interviewed!

Instructions
Ask another member of the class to be your partner. Audiotape each other as you review the preceding self-analysis. Play back the tape and offer suggestions about which answers sound most effective. Suggest areas that need to be explained more completely.

CHECKLIST

Before each interview:
    Review your self-analysis **out loud.**

☐	a. What are my interests?
☐	b. What are my short- and long-range career goals?
☐	c. What are my short- and long-range personal goals?
☐	d. What are my skills and assets?
☐	e. What are my strengths and weaknesses?

WORLD OF WORK   **What Else Does It Take?**

It is also important to know what else the interviewer will probably expect you to bring to the interview. For example, if you are a chef, it will be good to show the interviewer a portfolio of your recipes and menus, including photos of dishes you have prepared. If you developed special drawings and blueprints in your civil engineering program, take them with you. Review suggestions for constructing a portfolio in Chapter Two. Call the company before the interview to see what supplemental information will be useful to bring with you.

5.2 THE PREINTERVIEW PROCESS

No matter how many times you apply for a job, do not eliminate this part of the review process.

1. Plan your job hunting:
    a. Start the job search as soon as you know you will need to find a position.
    b. Plan your job hunt as a full-time project. You work a forty-hour week for an employer, and you should work no less for yourself.
    c. Once you start the job-finding campaign, do not allow yourself little vacations.
    d. Apply early enough in the day to allow sufficient time for multiple interviews, tests, or other hiring procedures that may be required.
    e. Learn everything you can about the company before you apply: size, products, types of clothing employees are expected to wear, average salary, hiring practices and policies.
    f. Know why you want to work for the firm.
    g. Follow up job leads immediately.
    h. If this company does not schedule appointments, find out the best time of day and the best day of the week to apply.
    i. If you learn of a job opening late in the day, call to arrange an appointment for the next day. They might postpone a hiring decision until you are interviewed.

2. Allow extra time to get to the interview. You never know when a train at a railroad crossing or a traffic roadblock could cause you to miss a valuable interview.

3. Go to the interview alone. Others could distract from what you have to say.

4. Do not carry packages with you. They, too, can become an awkward distraction. Carrying packages might give the impression that you are more interested in going shopping than in obtaining the job.

5. Men who are applying for a business position should wear a suit, shirt, and tie. Women also can wear a suit or a dress with a jacket. Neutral colors, conservative shoes, and tailored accessories are considered proper in most interview situations.

6. Some companies will not expect you to wear a business suit if you are applying for technical employment such as fluid power, electronics, carpentry, or welding, but wear clothing appropriate to the job. If you would be making service calls for this company, slacks and a shirt or blouse and maybe a jacket would be appropriate. Be neat, clean, well groomed and plan ahead of time what to wear.

7. Things to take with you to the interview:
   a. Your Social Security card
   b. Driver's license
   c. Military records
   d. School transcript
   e. Two pens—one black ink, one blue ink
   f. Pencils
   g. Extra paper and a calculator
   h. Money for bus fare or a telephone call
   i. Completed generic application form from Chapter Three
   j. Extra copies of your resume and your portfolio

The transcripts, extra paper, and application form could all be contained in a notebook or a nice folder with pockets.

8. Take any tools you might need to demonstrate your specific skills. For example, if you apply for a welding job, take your leathers and slag hammers with you.

9. Some organizations now require not only drug testing but also a history of your driving record as a condition for employment. Be prepared for these possibilities.

10. Some companies now require a fragrance-free environment. You may want to check on this situation prior to the interview.

5.3 INTERVIEW DO'S AND DON'T'S

Do

- Do arrive at least twenty minutes before the scheduled interview to fill out any needed application forms.
- Do write neatly on all application forms.
- Do remove your hat and comb your hair before the interview.
- Do look, feel, and act enthusiastic.
- Do believe in yourself, what you are doing, your education, your abilities, the company, and the job.
- Do emphasize your productivity and the quality of your work.
- Do sell yourself—let the interviewer know why you would be an asset to the company.
- Do sit up straight in your chair and lean slightly forward.
- Do keep your feet flat on the floor or cross your legs at the ankles. (Crossing your legs at the knees makes it too easy to jiggle your foot when you are nervous.)
- Do maintain direct eye contact with the interviewer to show interest and honesty.

Don't

- Don't sit down until you are invited to do so. Waiting to be seated shows respect.
- Don't smoke or drink coffee, even if they are offered. There is a chance you could spill the coffee. The offer of a cigarette could be a way of finding out if you smoke when the company maintains a smokeless environment.
- Don't eat anything unless the interview is conducted during a meal. In this situation, order something light.
- Don't drink alcoholic beverages before or during the interview!
- Don't put tools, a portfolio, or other materials on the interviewer's desk unless asked to do so.
- Don't lean on the interviewer's desk. The desk is the interviewer's personal space, and you don't want to "invade" it!
- Don't look around the room while the interviewer is talking.

Additional important things to remember are:

- Write down the names and positions of all the people you meet. A small pocket-sized (3 × 5) notebook is useful for this purpose.
- Use the interviewer's name when shaking hands, occasionally during the interview, and when leaving the room—for example, "I'm glad to meet you, Mrs. Owen," and "Thank you for your time, Mrs. Owen."
- Shake hands with both male *and* female interviewers, even if you are also a woman.
- Relax as you talk.
- Listen attentively to the interviewer instead of thinking about what you will say next.
- Reflect your energetic attitude by the way you walk into and out of the room, by your pleasant facial expression, and by your cheerful tone of voice.
- Sound enthusiastic. Employers say they want to interview people they can hear and who sound as if they will have enough energy to last the day!
- Reflect your eager attitude by choosing positive words.
- Be prepared to answer questions honestly and with more than a "yes" or "no."

5.4 TYPES OF INTERVIEWS

Depending on the nature of the job and the preferred style of interviewing, you may encounter various types of interview formats. An important component of job interviews in this country is to maintain direct eye contact between the interviewee and interviewer regardless of the format.

WORLD OF WORK A highly qualified young woman from the Philippines applied several times for various office technology positions in the United States, but was not hired. When she followed up on these interviews, she discovered that her poor eye contact was the primary factor contributing to the rejection. After discussing this revelation with her instructor, she was able to adjust her eye contact to a more direct Western style of nonverbal communication, even though, as she observed, "My grandmother would consider me to be very disrespectful if I looked her directly in the eyes, and she would spank me!"

Most interviews can be classified into one of five formats:

1. **One-on-one interviews:** In a one-on-one interview, you meet with one person at the company. The interview may be conducted by a personnel director as a screening interview and may involve questions to determine how well you fit into the company. You might be asked questions about your communication style or your problem-solving experiences. Sometimes you may be asked to demonstrate your computer or math skills.
   a. **The screening interview** is often used by large companies such as the Boeing Corporation and Hewlett Packard. After this interview, the personnel director may *then* refer you to the business office or the technical area relevant to your training.
   b. **Traits to communicate:**
      1. The ability to work independently *as well as* the ability to be part of a team
      2. The ability to solve problems
      3. The ability to communicate effectively
   c. **Suggestion:** Be ready to discuss specific examples of these abilities from previous work experiences and recent education.
2. **Technical interviews:** In a technical interview, you may be asked to explain schematics and/or diagrams. The interviewer may request that you demonstrate your skills with actual materials. For example, if you are a welder, you might be asked to show your ability to weld in several positions.
   Because you never know if you will encounter this type of interview, be sure to take your tools with you to all interviews.
   a. **The technical interview** is usually conducted in a shop or on the line by a specialist in the field. It could be a hands-on display of your skills.
   b. **The most important traits** to display in this type of interview are:
      1. Honesty: If you don't know about something or can't solve the problem in the schematic, say so!
      2. Staying calm under pressure. If you get confused at some point, back up and start over.

      c. Suggestion: Because employers often want to see how you will respond in an actual work setting, be willing to say, "I don't know," rather than pretend you know an answer.

3. **Team interviews:** Team interviews are conducted by two to five people as a group. This type of interview may be done in person, or you might be involved in a conference telephone call. The conference call would connect you with either a few people sitting around a table and taking turns asking questions, or one person is asking questions while the others listen and make notes.

    Team interviews also may be conducted sequentially. The interviewee will meet with two to five people, one right after the other.

      a. Team interviews are frequently used by companies who have an established group in place and want to see how you will fit in with that team.

      b. The key here is to be yourself, not what you think the team is looking for. The traits to communicate, again, are:
        1) Honesty
        2) Flexibility

      c. Suggestion: Be careful of overtalking and overanswering questions. Too much information can disrupt the timing of the interview.

4. **Social interviews:** Social interviews are held during lunch or breakfast, or in some other informal setting:

      a. The social interview is used to relax people and let the employer get to know the "real you." These may be the last in a series of interviews, but could be the first depending on the company and type of job. This style of interviewing is sometimes used by companies looking for people who will need to have social contact with potential and present customers.

      b. The ability to demonstrate effective customer relations is essential. Give examples of how you calmed an irate customer or sold a product if that is part of your past experience.

      c. Suggestions: Because this type of interview is often used to determine how well you fit socially within the work group, it is important to remember that although this is a social situation, it is still

an interview! Be friendly and outgoing, but do not speak or act unprofessionally at any time. Dress appropriately. If you are not sure what to wear, wear the most conservative option you are considering. Order a light meal. Stick to nonalcoholic beverages.

5. **Office or shop interviews:** These interviews usually involve touring the office or shop with the interviewer, observing operations, and asking questions. This type of interview demonstrates your understanding of the purpose of the business. You may also be asked to demonstrate your problem-solving skills in an unfamiliar environment.

    a. **The office or shop interview** is usually conducted by the office manager, line supervisor, or shop foreman to see how much you know about the company and the type of work they do.

    b. **The traits to demonstrate** in this situation are:

      1. Your knowledge of the company

      2. Interest in the operations, expressed by making observations and asking thoughtful questions

    c. **Suggestions:** Maintain a professional attitude by being positive about the company while avoiding being overly critical of their competitors.

Be prepared for more than one type of interview. People in many career areas will first have a personnel screening interview, followed by a technical, office, or shop interview. However, three or four interviews may be conducted, depending on the responsibility level of the position.

TOOLS OF COMMUNICATION

Personal Skills

Instructions
Pick your strongest skill or the personal attribute you most want to emphasize during your next job interview. Think of specific examples of situations in which you demonstrated this skill. Describe how you might discuss it in two of the interview formats you will most likely encounter.

Interview Format: Screening Interview
How could you emphasize your skill in problem solving when working with people? Use specific examples.

Interview Format: Office or Technical Interview
How could you emphasize your problem-solving skill with specific examples?

5.7 INTERVIEW STRUCTURE

The interview style combined with the different types of questions produces the overall structure of the interview. Most interviews contain four basic parts. The following interview usually takes 30 to 40 minutes.

Opening

The opening of the interview involves greeting and getting acquainted. You and the interviewer become comfortable with each other. Remember that hiring decisions are often made during the first 90 seconds of an interview, and 30 to 70 percent of those decisions are based on nonverbal communication! Pay attention to your handshake, eye contact, even how you walk and sit. Do not be too relaxed, but do not perch like a bird on the edge of your chair.

> **Time:** 30 seconds to 2 minutes
>
> **Purpose:** Break the ice, become comfortable with each other.
>
> **Possible content:** Interviewer will welcome you, ask you to sit down, exchange of names, chitchat about the weather, and so on.

Introduction

During the introduction, the interviewer explains the position and the company. The introduction usually involves the topics that will be discussed, when the hiring decision will be made, and the requirements for the job.

Be sure to listen carefully so you do not ask questions about something that was explained in the introduction. This could be a good time to mention your portfolio if you have brought one.

> **Time:** 1 to 3 minutes
>
> **Purpose:** Give you the basic information about the interview.
>
> **Possible content:** Brief overview of the company, positions available, ground rules for the interview.

Body

The body of the interview involves three parts:

1. **Exploration:** First, the interviewer will explore your background, personal strengths and weaknesses, knowledge of the position and of the organization, and values and priorities that could affect your work. The interviewer wants to know about factors that would influence your job satisfaction. The employer also wants to be assured you are really willing to work, not just show up.

Time: 10 to 20 minutes

Purpose: Identify your values, education, experience, and priorities relating to job performance.

> Compare your strengths with the demands of the job.
>
> See if you have a realistic view of the position and the company.
>
> Determine your level of self-knowledge.
>
> Predict your success as an employee.

Possible content: Questions concerning:

> Your grades, internships, activities, coursework, and work experience.
>
> Your self-description, involving your preferences relating to activities.
>
> Types of problems you have encountered and how they were solved.
>
> Your job qualifications and interest in the company.
>
> Your future goals, including keys to success in the organization.
>
> Factors affecting your job satisfaction.
>
> Your ethics and personal values.

WORLD OF WORK   When discussing personal values and priorities, do not tell an interviewer what one carpentry student said, "I would rather do framing than finish work because I can hide my mistakes."

---

2. **Your questions:** The interviewer will usually ask if you have any questions. Be sure to have some prepared (see Section 5.7 in this chapter for questions to ask during an interview).

   Time: 1 to 2 minutes

   Purpose: Give you a chance to learn information that has not been covered and to clarify any of your concerns that may have occurred during the interview.

   Possible content: Your questions should relate to the job description and job priorities, but not to money or benefits, unless you have been offered the position. You should already know about the salary and benefits because of the company research you conducted prior to the interview.

3. **Identifying next steps:** Finally, the interviewer will probably tell you what to expect next in the interviewing process. For example, the interviewer may tell you whether you will be called or if you should telephone for the results of the interview. Make sure to ask about the decision-making process if the interviewer does not give you this information.

   Time: 1 to 2 minutes

   Purpose: Inform you of the next steps in the interview or offer you a position.

   Possible content: The interviewer will state how and when the company will contact you. The interviewer may ask you to call back at a certain time. Be sure to make notes so you can write an appropriate thank you letter.

WORLD OF WORK   Be diplomatic when you clarify the final steps of your interviewing process. Saying "I want to work for your company" is appropriate. But saying, "My goal is to sit where you are sitting!" was viewed by one interviewer as being too aggressive. Remember, your purpose for the interview is to obtain a job offer; whether or not you decide to accept it is another issue. Another interviewer said the question, "How soon can I start?" was too pushy. A possible way to inquire about the next steps politely could be, "When will you make your hiring decision?"

Closing

The closing involves your leaving the interview. Always shake hands when you leave and thank the interviewer for his or her time, even if you do not think the interview was successful. Make sure to leave promptly when you sense that the interview is over.

> **Time:** 30 seconds
>
> **Purpose:** End the interview pleasantly and promptly
>
> **Possible content:** The interviewer may put your resume aside, look at the clock, stand up, or say thank you for coming.

The preceding format is the basic outline for an interview. A good interviewer will move through each of these stages with ease. A poor interviewer may get stuck or lost in one of the stages. If this happens, you may have to take some initiative and tactfully redirect the discussion.

This exercise provides experience in a critical phase of the employment process. Even if you have been interviewed dozens of times, try this exercise to further sharpen your communication tools.

TOOLS OF COMMUNICATION

Screening Interview

Instructions

A short, structured interview is often used by personnel departments when screening applicants for various departments. It usually takes 10 or 15 minutes.

1. Visualize a specific company you would like to work for, write a job description that would be applicable to your field of study, and select six to eight of the questions on pages 141 and 142.

2. Work with a partner and interview each other using the outlines you just developed.

3. Have your partner audiotape your responses or, preferably, videotape this practice interview.

4. Now, play back the tape. Both of you evaluate each other and yourselves according to the rating sheet on page 140.

5. Compare your evaluations.

6. What are your strengths?

7. How could you improve your answers the next time?

8. Did your answers give specific examples of work you have done?

Most responses should be a minute or two in length. Do not overtalk and bore the interviewer or try to take control of the interview.

If you are working alone, ask the questions of yourself and answer them out loud while you audio tape yourself. Then play back the tape and evaluate yourself. Another option would be to write out your answers in the space provided to get a visual picture of what you want to say.

ANSWERING INTERVIEW QUESTIONS

Interviewee: _____

Your Name: _____

	Fair 3	Good 4	Excellent 5
1. Wording the answer:			
Used complete sentences			
Positive answer			
Was specific			
2. Nonverbal message:			
Posture			
Facial expressions			
Eye contact			
Hands and gestures			
Legs and feet			
3. Voice:			
Volume			
Interest and enthusiasm			
Sounded positive			
Energy level			
Total			
4. Comments:			

Interviewer's Introduction

The purpose of this interview is to gather data pertinent to an interest in employment that you may have with our company. As we proceed, we will not delve too much into the actual specifics of your skills or trade(s). That will be accomplished at a later interview. We are looking for information about you. Do you have any questions before we proceed?

1. What kind of work would you most like to do for our company?

2. Please describe any activities which have provided you with experiences, training or skills which you feel will help you in the position you are applying for.

3. Are there certain activities you feel more confident performing than others? What are they and why do you feel that way?

4. Tell me about your last or present job, describing what you did, what were your major responsibilities, and describe a typical day.

   Of the responsibilities you mentioned, which presented the most difficulty for you?

5. What were some of the problems you encountered in performing your last job and how did you overcome them?

6. What is your real career objective? What have you done or intend to do outside of your job to help you reach this objective?

7. We are looking for employees with a commitment to this position. Are there any reasons why you might not stay with us?

8. Do you have any commitments which would prevent you from working regular hours?

   Are you available to work overtime, if needed?

IF YES, are there any limitations or restrictions on your ability to work overtime?

9. Do you have any health conditions which would prevent you from performing all the duties of this job?

10. What was your absentee record at your prior place of employment? Or at school?

11. Do you anticipate missing work days because of any health condition?

12. What is your strongest personal quality or qualification? Why?

13. What is your weakest area? Why?

14. What specific job factors are important to you?

15. What job factors would you like to avoid in a job? Why?

16. Are there any other factors that we have not discussed that make you uniquely qualified for this position?

Structured Screening Interview Format developed by John Goetz, Human Resources Department, Community Colleges of Spokane, Spokane, WA. Used by permission.

5.6 ANSWERING INTERVIEW QUESTIONS EFFECTIVELY

Prior to the interview, it's a good idea to practice answering many different types of questions aloud. Watch yourself in the mirror, and keep listening to yourself on audio tape. If possible, have someone videotape you in a practice interview so you can evaluate the total impression you make. Ask others to evaluate how you come across by using the interview evaluation forms provided later in this chapter. The more you practice answering questions, the more confident you will feel during the actual interview.

Most interviewers have a set of standard questions, but not all interviewers are trained in effective interviewing. Therefore, you need to know how to respond to vague or even illegal questions. You also will need to answer difficult questions about your background with honesty and confidence and be prepared to explain how you have overcome any past difficulties.

Answering Standard Interview Questions

Open-Ended Questions

When using this type of question, interviewers expect you to organize your thoughts and give them detailed information on a variety of topics. An example of an open question is: "Tell me about your training." Practice how you will respond to open-ended questions by providing specific information highlighting those skills and experience that make you the best candidate for the job. For example:

> **Interviewer:** Tell me about your work experience.
>
> **Efficient response:** I started working on the family farm while I was still in high school and learned to repair and operate the equipment in all types of weather, because when the crops are ready to harvest you don't take the day off. Since I've been in school, I'm working part time to help the instructor in his own machine shop on weekends and in the evenings.
>
> **Inefficient response:** I worked on the family farm and part time while I'm in school.

Sometimes customer relations problems may be included in open-ended types of questions. For example:

> **Interviewer:** What would you say if an old customer came in and demanded you work on his computer project immediately, but you are already working on another job?
>
> **Efficient response:** "I'll be glad to help you when I finish this job I'm working on right now. That will probably be in about an hour. Do you want to wait and have a cup of coffee, or do you want to come back later? I can call your office when I'm ready for your project."
>
> **Inefficient response:** "I'm busy, you'll have to wait your turn."

Be prepared for technical or problem-solving open-ended questions that are specific to your specialized training. For example:

> **Interviewer:** Please show me (while displaying a schematic) where the problem is in this diagram.
>
> **Efficient response:** I can trace the problem to here, but I'm not sure where to go next.
>
> **Inefficient response:** The person who drew this diagram must have made a mistake. No circuit should be designed like this.

Being honest about what you know and don't know is much preferred to bluffing your way through the problem-solving process.

Closed Questions

When using closed questions, interviewers usually focus their questions on specific subjects. Those questions generally can be answered with one or two words. An example of a closed question is:

> *"Did you like your previous employer?'*

To give the interviewer a better understanding of your abilities, you need to expand your answer rather than using just one or two words. It takes time and practice to learn how to answer closed questions with more than a "yes" or "no" answer. For example:

> **Interviewer:** Did you like your last job?
>
> **Efficient response:** Yes, I enjoyed the people I worked with at Smith Company, as well as the challenges of finding ways to solve the customers' problems.
>
> **Inefficient response:** Yes.

Always use actual examples of how you accomplished a task or demonstrated a skill. This type of a response will give the interviewer a more complete picture of who you are than a simple "yes" or "no" answer.

Paraphrasing Vague Questions

The paraphrasing and listening tools discussed in Chapter Four are essential skills to use during job interviews. Some employers are not experienced interviewers, and their questions can be vague or general. The key communication tool to apply in this case is to paraphrase in order to clarify the vague question. For example:

> **Interviewer:** Tell me, Susan, what do you like to do?
>
> **Efficient response:** I have several interests, Mr. Jones. Would you like to know about my problem-solving efforts at work or about my computer skills?
>
> **Inefficient response:** What do you mean?

The efficient response paraphrases the interviewer's question, is more detailed, and helps the interviewer focus on the information he or she really wants to know. Because the interviewee phrased the answer in the form of a clarifying question, the interviewer is still in control of the situation. The inefficient response could put the interviewer on the spot and make him or her feel defensive.

TOOLS OF COMMUNICATION

Paraphrasing Questions to Your Advantage

Instructions
Work with a partner who will take the role of an interviewer. Then reverse positions so each of you can practice clarifying these open-ended questions quickly and efficiently. Paraphrase to help the interviewer focus on facts and ideas you want to discuss. Practice giving your response verbally to your partner. Audio or video tape each other, if possible.

If you have difficulty wording your responses, write them out and then practice them out loud.

If you are working on this without a partner, you can still follow the same procedure. In this situation, audio and/or video taping your responses will be especially useful because you can see and hear how others might perceive you.

1. **Interviewer:** What have you done that shows initiative?

   Your response:

2. **Interviewer:** How do you define *success?*

   Your response:

3. **Interviewer:** What are your goals?

   Your response:

Redirecting Irrelevant or Illegal Questions

Another tool for answering questions successfully is called **redirecting.** This technique is especially useful if an employer rambles on about irrelevant topics or asks illegal questions. Redirecting a question involves carefully and diplomatically turning the question away from the irrelevant or illegal topic and rephrasing it to highlight your skills. The goal is not to take control away from the interviewer, but to keep the focus on why you are the best person for the job.

Irrelevant Questions
Practice redirecting irrelevant questions. For example, the following question has nothing to do with the job:

> **Interviewer:** Ron, I see you're from the northwest. I just read a book about Alaska. Have you ever been there?

> **Efficient response:** Yes, it's wonderful. I enjoyed going there with my family three years ago during a vacation. This gave me time to evaluate

my priorities and set some employment goals. In fact, that's when I decided to get some advanced computer training and on the use of the machines like the ones you have here in the office.

Inefficient response: Yeah, I went there with my family.

Note that even an irrelevant question can be used to introduce information about job-related skills!

Illegal Questions

According to the Federal Equal Employment Opportunity Act, most questions about religion, marital status, children, age, place of birth, race, and ethnic background are **not legal** during an interview. If you are asked a question about one of these topics, you may answer it if you choose to do so. However, you can redirect the questions by asking how that information would affect this job. If the employer does have valid reasons for asking this type of question, offer a short, focused answer. If the question is asked with a hidden motive or simply out of curiosity, redirecting the question will probably cause the interviewer to drop the topic.

You do not have to answer the question, "Have you ever been arrested?" However, you must truthfully answer the question, "Have you ever been convicted of a felony?"

Practice redirecting an illegal question. For example:

Interviewer: Sally, I see on your application that you have two children. Who's going to take care of the children while you're at work? (This question is illegal. The interviewer has no right to ask about Sally's family status.)

Efficient response: I have made child care arrangements. The children will not affect my availability to work, even to work overtime when necessary. In fact, during the two years I was getting my training I never missed a class because of problems with child care.

Inefficient response: That's none of your business!

TOOLS OF COMMUNICATION

Redirecting Questions

Instructions
Practice redirecting questions by writing your answers to these questions. Share your ideas with the class.

1. **Interviewer:** What did you think about your training? (Vague)

   Your response:

2. **Interviewer:** How old are you? (This is usually illegal unless you would be serving liquor or for insurance purposes.)

   Your response:

3. **Interviewer:** What nationality is your name? (This is illegal.)

   Your response:

Answering Difficult Questions

Difficult questions include questions about employment gaps in your resume, frequent job changes, time spent in jail, or lack of much work experience. Take the initiative to talk about difficult questions in a straightforward manner.

Here are several other difficult questions and sample responses.

Interviewer: Have you ever been convicted of a felony?

Efficient response: Yes, but I was younger [state how old you were if that is relevant], and actually this turned out for the best. I faced the results of my bad choices and turned my life in a positive direction by going back to school.

Inefficient response: Yes [with no explanation].

Interviewer: Have you ever been injured?

Efficient response: Yes, but since I've been cross-trained, I haven't had a problem with attendance at my technical training.

or

I was, but since then I have chosen a different career and I have experienced no physical limitations.

Inefficient response: Yes, I had a back injury when I worked at the mill.

Interviewer: You are retiring from the military. You must only want a part-time position.

Efficient response: Absolutely not! I am looking forward to the challenge of a career change and will enjoy this opportunity to develop another part of my life.

Inefficient response: Yes, I put in my twenty years.

TOOLS OF COMMUNICATION

Difficult Questions

Instructions

Practice answering difficult questions. Make your answers honest, straightforward, and positive. Practice giving your responses aloud with a partner. Then trade places. Audio or video tape yourself if possible. If you have difficulty wording your responses, write them first, and then practice them out loud.

1. Interviewer: Why did you leave your last job?

Your response:

2. Interviewer: What kind of a person annoys you?

Your response:

3. Interviewer: What part of your technical training would you change?

Your response:

Remember to be careful of criticism. Criticism of a former employer or instructor during a job interview usually indicates a negative attitude on your part, and most employers do not want to hire someone with a negative attitude. When you are asked why you left a job, state your answer calmly, briefly, and truthfully—for example, "I left my previous position because I no longer felt that my responsibilities provided the challenges that I look for in a job." Do not say, "The boss was a jerk!" or "I didn't get along with my instructor!"

5.7 ASKING PRODUCTIVE QUESTIONS

WORLD OF WORK Linn Fyhrie, a line supervisor for the Hewlett Packard Company, states that when a potential employee asks specific questions about the objectives and needs of his company, it is a positive factor in the interviewee's favor. It is always productive to form questions demonstrating interest in and knowledge of the company where you are applying. Different types of questions are appropriate at different times during the interviewing process.

Questions to ask before you are offered the job:
1. Do you have an education/training program? Please describe it.
2. What specific responsibilities are trainees given?
3. What percentage of your leadership openings are filled from within?
4. Did my resume raise any questions that I can answer?
5. Are there some negative aspects to the job you are offering?
6. Would you please describe the duties (or responsibilities) of the job (if they have not been explained).
7. Was the person who previously held this job promoted?
8. Could you please tell me about the people I would be working with?
9. What is the single largest problem facing your department [staff or crew] now?
10. Will there be an opportunity for advancement?
11. What personal tools would be required for this job?
12. How often are employees evaluated? At what intervals are written performance evaluations given?

Questions to ask after the employer has offered you the job:
1. Could you please tell me about the benefits of the company? (You really should have investigated and should know this information before applying for the job.)
2. Are there investment options?
3. If you are moving to another area, "What's the cost of living and the housing situation where I'd be employed?"

Questions to ask if you don't get the job:
1. Are there others in the organization who might be interested in someone with my qualifications and experience?
2. Do you know of another company that is looking for someone with my skills?
3. Do you have any suggestions for improving my resume or interviewing skills for my next interview?

Questions to ask if the interviewer is undecided:
1. When will a decision be made?
2. May I call you later in the week? (Depending on the response to #1.)
3. What time or day would be convenient for me to call?

TOOLS OF COMMUNICATION

What Do You Want to Know?

Develop a list of five questions that you would like to ask the interviewer at your next job interview, such as:

1. What additional computer skills would you suggest for this position?

2. What "people" skills will someone in this position need to use?

3. Do you foresee any reorganization in your company in the near future?

4.

5.

6.

7.

8.

5.8 FINISHING WITH FLAIR AND FOLLOWING UP

Congratulations! You made it through the interview! However, you cannot afford to sit back and relax while waiting for the phone to ring with the news that you got the job. You are now in the follow-up phase of the interview process. Interview follow-up is important to your success in getting a job because it provides one more opportunity to let employers know you are interested in their employment opportunity. Even if you do not want to work there, an expression of appreciation for the time spent with you will help to maintain your network of employers. The first thing you need to do in this follow-up process is to write a thank you letter to the interviewer(s).

Thank you letters should be written on the same day as the interview, while you are still feeling enthusiastic (or depressed) and can remember details. Nervousness or mistakes made during the interview can also be discussed in a thank you letter.

An effective thank you letter will contain the following steps, but not necessarily in this order:

1. An expression of your gratitude for the interview, including the date of the interview
2. The position for which you were interviewed
3. A reminder of two or three of your specific skills relating to the opening
4. A summary statement of your interest in the job, including your telephone number
5. A complimentary closing

Thank You Letters

Thank you letters are an important first thing to do in the follow-up process! One applicant took the time to thank the interviewer in writing even though she did not get the job she had applied for. When the newly hired employee was fired, the woman who had written the letter was offered the position. The employer said that she had demonstrated good attention to details by taking the time to write the letter, and that attention to details was a vital quality in this career.

SAMPLE THANK YOU FOR THE INTERVIEW LETTER
WHEN THE INTERVIEWEE WAS ASKED TO A FOLLOW-UP

Route 2, Box 104A
Cheney, WA 99004
May 27, 1996

Mr. Tom Neuman
Personnel Manager
Daytron Corporation
PO Box 14687
Spokane, WA 99214

Dear Mr. Neuman:

I would like you to know how much I appreciated being interviewed by you yesterday for the fluid power position.

I believe my background with the military, which included work in hydraulics, pneumatics, and management, in conjunction with training in Fluid Power Technology at Spokane Community College, has prepared me for the work we discussed.

I am looking forward to being associated with Daytron Corporation in its growth as it develops the new plant in Cheney.

I will be contacting you June 15, as you requested, regarding employment with Daytron at the Cheney location. My message phone is 328-4250 if you need to talk to me before that date. Thank you, once again, for your time and consideration.

Sincerely yours,

Charles V. Hayord

Charles V. Hayord
CVH/bjr

East 12702 Hale
Greeley, CO 83815
December 14, 1995

Ms. Ester Boyd, Director
Human Resources
Nighthawk Corporation
2711 Brighton St.
Denver, CO 47836

Dear Ms. Boyd:

I appreciated the opportunity to talk with you December 12th about the computer programming position. The prospect of working with the Nighthawk Corporation is exciting. I was pleased that the problem-solving skills developed at the Cole's Company and my education at Weld County Community College are so close to the qualifications you described.

It was also helpful for me to meet Mr. Fisher, who is in charge of the lab. The time he took to give me a tour of the lab was very helpful. Please express my thanks to him as well.

You may call (567) 928-0248 between 8:00 A.M. and 5:00 P.M. regarding this position. I will look forward to hearing from you.

Sincerely,

Charles B. Hibbert

Charles B. Hibbert

TOOLS OF COMMUNICATION

Thank You Letters

Instructions

1. Develop two "Thank you for the interview" letters, one for each of the following situations:

   a. You were asked to call back to find out the company's decision.

   b. You were not asked to call back, perhaps made a mistake, omitted vital information about your background, or were overly nervous.

2. These two letters can be addressed to someone who interviewed you.

3. Ask someone else who is trained in writing skills to evaluate your letters using the following rating form. This person could be a fellow student, instructor, or friend. Be certain the person has current and accurate knowledge of business letters.

4. After you receive feedback from someone else, revise and correct the letters and keep them in a folder for use following future job interviews.

RATING THE THANK YOU FOR THE INTERVIEW LETTER

	Possible Points out of 100	Your letter's score
1. Thank you	10	
2. Date of interview	10	
3. Name of position	10	
4. Your skills related to the job, and/or clear up any errors made during the interview	20	
5. Statement of interest in the job	10	
6. Your telephone number	10	
7. Complimentary closing	5	
8. Neatness and alignment	5	
9. Correct spelling, punctuation, and sentence structure	20	

Follow-up Self-Analysis

Think about what you can do to improve your next interview. Analyze the questions you asked and the answers you gave at your last interview. Ask yourself:

1. Did I have enough information about the company?
2. Did my skills and abilities match the job description?
3. Did I need to share more specific examples from previous work experiences?
4. Did I talk too long or not long enough?
5. Did I sound enthusiastic?
6. Did I use effective nonverbal communication skills?

Follow Up by Keeping a Log

Remember to keep all job information confidential until you get the job. You may create unnecessary competition for yourself by discussing the job opening with others.

1. After an interview, it is helpful to keep a notebook of the dates of the interviews, including the names and positions of anyone you spoke to. This is especially important for future correspondence.
2. Writing another follow-up letter a week or two after your first thank you letter will demonstrate continued interest in the job. Even if the position is filled by someone else, you never know when another opportunity with that employer may occur.

Finally, don't stop looking for work while you wait for an answer from one company. Keep looking for employment with other companies until you receive a job offer!

Whether you are chosen for the job or not, remain confident, positive, and enthusiastic. Know that soon you will be hired for a job that's right for you!

WORLD OF WORK   ## Sure, I Want the Job

An article in *USA Today* (July 18, 1989), described a survey conducted by Robert Half, president of the research firm Robert Half International. He surveyed 100 personnel directors to find out the kinds of crazy things people do and say during job interviews.

Here are some examples:

"Dozed off and started snoring during the interview."

"Wore a Walkman and said she could listen to me and the music at the same time."

"Interrupted to phone his therapist for advice on answering specific interview questions."

"Brought her large dog to the interview."

"Stretched out on the floor to fill out the job application."

The most important thing to do during a job interview, Half says, is the easiest: *Be nice.* An interview is a tense situation, so *try to think of the word "smile."*

STRESS LESS   ## Learning to Say No

When you are looking for employment, you do not have the time to help everyone who needs your assistance, so you need to learn how to say no in a positive way. Try responding to requests this way: "I would really like to help you, but I have to get ready for a job interview. Maybe we can get together on Sunday afternoon."

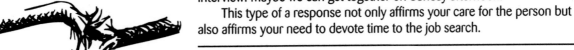

This type of a response not only affirms your care for the person but also affirms your need to devote time to the job search.

CASE STUDY   *Harold and Shawn are both applying for the same position with a local manufacturing company. The position will require some travel to do equipment maintenance and some bench work in the shop. Each applicant has completed the same technical training with similar grades at the same community college.*

Harold has recently returned to the civilian work force after spending twenty years in the navy, where he had some experience doing electronic maintenance work aboard ships.

Shawn completed his technical training right after graduating from high school and held a part-time job for an auto parts store during high school and college.

Discuss this situation in small groups, and have someone record the group's answers. Share the observations later with the class. List each group's answers on the board.

1. *What are Harold's strengths? His weaknesses?*
2. *What are Shawn's strengths? His weaknesses?*
3. *As a team, decide which one you would hire, and explain why.*

If you are working on this case study alone, follow the same procedure.

CHAPTER PROJECT   **Interviewing in Teams**

Instructions

Work in teams of three to five people. Use the format for the detailed interview on pages 137–139, and choose eight to ten questions from pages 154–156 following these instructions. Develop an outline for an interview for your technical field. Conduct an interview for each member of the team. Audiotape the interview or, preferably, videotape it. Evaluate the nonverbal communication, and note appropriate answers and areas that still need improvement. Be sure everyone has an opportunity to be both an interview*er* and an interview*ee*. One team member can operate the video equipment, while other team members will be the evaluators, again using the evaluation form on page 156.

Questions rated **excellent** will have detailed answers with job-specific examples.

Questions rated **good** will involve less detail and fewer examples.

Questions rated **fair** will be shorter and have only one or two examples.

Questions rated **poor** will be primarily yes or no answers and contain no specific examples.

If you are working alone, write out your answers to the following questions. Then audio and/or video tape your responses, play them back, and evaluate yourself. You could also benefit from having a friend, fellow student, or co-worker evaluate your tape and offer feedback about your interviewing strengths and weaknesses.

Here are some questions frequently asked by employers during interviews. What would be your answers?

1. What are your future plans in this technical field?
2. How do you spend your spare time? What are your hobbies?
3. In what type of position are you most interested?
4. Why do you think you might like to work for our company?
5. What jobs have you held? How were they obtained, and why did you leave?
6. What courses did you like best? Least? Why?
7. Why did you choose your particular field of work?
8. What do you know about our company?
9. Do you feel that you have received a good general training?
10. What qualifications do you have that make you feel that you could be successful in your field?

11. What are your ideas on salary?

12. If you were starting your training all over again, what courses would you take?

13. Can you forget your education and start from scratch?

14. Do you prefer any specific geographic location? Why?

15. Why did you decide to go to this particular school?

16. What do you think determines a person's progress in a good company?

17. What personal characteristics are necessary for success in your chosen field?

18. Why do you think you would like this particular type of job?

19. Do you prefer working with others or by yourself?

20. What kind of boss do you prefer?

21. Can you take instructions without feeling upset?

22. Tell me about an experience that has affected your life.

23. How did previous employers treat you?

24. What have you learned from some of the jobs you have held?

25. Can you get recommendations from previous employers?

26. What interests you about our product or service?

27. Since this job creates a lot of stress, what do you do to reduce stress?

28. Have you ever changed your major field of interest while in college? Why?

29. Do you feel you have done the best scholastic work of which you are capable?

30. What do you know about opportunities in the field for which you are trained?

31. How long do you expect to work for us?

32. Have you ever had any difficulty getting along with fellow students and/or faculty?

33. What are your plans for furthering your education?

34. Do you like routine work?

35. Do you like regular hours?

36. Define *cooperation* and give an example of when you demonstrated this quality.

37. Will you fight to get ahead?

38. Do you have an analytical mind?

39. Are you eager to please?

40. Have you had any serious illness or injury?

41. What job in our company would you choose if you were entirely free to do so?

42. Is it an effort for you to be tolerant of persons with a background and interests different from your own? Give an example of how you worked out those differences.

43. What types of people seem to "rub you the wrong way"?

44. What jobs have you enjoyed the most? Least? Why?

45. What are your own special abilities?

46. Would you prefer a large or a small company? Why?

47. What is your idea of how industry operates today?

48. Do you like to travel?

49. How about overtime work?

50. What are the disadvantages of your chosen field?

51. Do you think that grades should be considered by employers? Why or why not?

52. Are you interested in research?

53. What have you done which shows initiative and willingness to work?

Note: If you will take the time necessary to write out brief answers to each of the questions in this list, it will help you to clarify your own thinking and establish ready answers.

Adapted from *Job Finding Kit,* published by the Coordinating Council for Occupational Education.

Evaluator: _____

Interview Evaluation Form

Interviewee: _____ Date: _____

	POOR	FAIR	GOOD	EXCELLENT
1. Opening:				
2. Describing background: • Tied in direct and indirect job-related experience to job description. • Tied academic background to job opening.				
3. Shows professional attitude:				
4. Interview preparation: • Knowledge of the company • Knowledge of the position				
5. Career objectives clear and realistic:				
6. Personal appearance:				
7. Self-confidence: • Believed in own ability. • Was positive about self.				
8. Positive verbal communication: • Answered questions quickly. • Used overview statements, then developed specifics. • Turned negative points into assets.				
9. Positive nonverbal communication:				
10. Revealed dynamic personal energy:				
11. Overall rating for interview:				

This exercise can be conducted in front of the entire class or used as a team project. The instructor also evaluates the in-class demonstration or the tapes and provides individual feedback.

Video Self-Analysis

Name_____

This self-analysis is worth 25 points and is due on the day of your scheduled playback. Be sure to bring your videotape to the playback session.

Instructions
Watch your videotaped interview and evaluate it using the form on p. 156 in this chapter, then answer the following questions:

Write a short paragraph answering the following questions:

1. What did you like best about how you responded to the interviewer? Be specific.

2. What did you like least about how you responded to the interviewing situation? Again, be specific.

3. What specific changes would you make in your next interview?

DISCUSSION QUESTIONS

1. What questions would you want to include in a job interview if you were the employer?
2. Which type of interview do you think is the most valuable—one on one, technical team, social, office, or shop? Why?
3. How would you rate the importance of eye contact during a job interview on a scale of 1 to 5 (1 is low and 5 is high) Why?
4. Which three questions do you believe are the most useful to *ask* a potential employer?

SUMMARY

In this chapter you learned about:

- Self-analysis and self-evaluation forms for each phase of the preinterview, interview, and follow-up process
- Factors employers consider important during job interviews
- Factors that can affect the job interview negatively
- Various interviewing formats
- Different types of interviewing questions
- Efficient and inefficient answers to questions
- A detailed screening interview
- Thank you for the interview letters

CHAPTER SIX

Communicating Effectively with External Customers

LEARNING OBJECTIVES

1. Understand the differences between internal and external customers.
2. Learn how to remember customers' names.
3. Discover customers' wants and needs.
4. Learn how perception affects productive communication with customers.
5. Practice the skill of perception checking.
6. Practice communicating with customers on the phone.
7. Learn how to communicate with critical customers.
8. Understand some cultural differences.
9. Practice giving oral sales, service, or technical report.

Once you are employed, it is vital to focus on communicating effectively with customers. Currently, customers are defined as both *external* and *internal*. The *external* customers are those who do *not* work for the company, and the *internal* customers are those who work *within* the company. The internal customers are more commonly known as your co-workers.

In his book *Customer Comes Second*, Hall Rosenbluth points out the need to maintain healthy communication within the business in order to preserve a productive environment. Smooth relationships internally usually will achieve positive results externally.

This chapter discusses the specific communication tools most useful when communicating with external customers. Chapter 7 will provide some guidelines for working effectively with co-workers in groups.

The 1998 survey of 200 employers in the northwestern United States stressed the importance of customer relations. In fact, 47.3 percent of these employers said the one thing that could get an employee fired was the inability to get along with external customers.

WORLD OF WORK   "In an amazing number of companies whose front-line workers have some interaction with customers, communication skill isn't a nice to have; it's a must have," says AEA's Fields-Tyler. (Jacobs, B5)

Why do external customers quit doing business with a company?

According to previous research, over half of them quit because of the indifferent attitude toward them by some employees.

Good service is an important aspect of relating to external customers. This can be accomplished by:

1. Knowing what the customer wants and needs
2. Using the correct communication tools necessary to meet those needs and wants

6.1 WHAT DO CUSTOMERS WANT?

In general, external customers look for businesses who will give them good feelings and/or solve their problems.

WORLD OF WORK   One thing that will help a customer to feel good is to be identified by the correct name.

At an office, one customer was mistakenly called by the wrong name twice. *Two years later*, she was still telling others about the incompetence of the people in that office—just because someone spoke to her using an incorrect name!

Remembering another person's name is a valuable tool that is really worth learning. A person's name is his or her badge of individuality. A name is important! Using customers' names lets them know you are really interested in them.

How to Remember Names

Try using the following four points in order to remember names more easily.

1. **Be really interested** . . . You must *really* want to improve your ability to remember names before you will make any progress.
2. **Impression** . . . It is important to get a clear impression of a name before you can hope to remember it!
   a. Listen to the name carefully when you are being introduced.
      (1) Ask to have the name repeated if you did not understand it.
      (2) Ask to have the name spelled, and write it down for a visual image.
   b. Get a vivid impression of the person.
      (1) Note the face and physical characteristics of the person.
      (2) Get a distinct impression of the voice.
3. **Repeat** . . . You will have less trouble remembering a name if you repeat it often enough.
   a. Repeat the name right after hearing it.
   b. Use the customer's name several times during the conversation.
   c. Work with *only a few names at a time, and repeat them to yourself several times before trying to add more names.*
4. **Relate** . . . Form a connection between the face impression and some mental picture the name suggests, such as "Fred Small is tall."
   a. Make a definite association such as, "Ted Ford drives a Chevy."
   b. The association may be made by linking the name with one of the following:
      (1) What the person does: *Ron works at the "Bon."*
      (2) Rhyme: *Sally, alley.*

TOOLS OF COMMUNICATION

Remembering Names

Instructions
Work in pairs.

1. Make up names and descriptions for each of the following five faces.

2. Exchange books.

3. Use the four-step process in *How to Remember Names.*

4. Take ten minutes to learn your partner's customers' names. Close the book.

5. List the names on a separate sheet of paper without looking at your partner's book.

6. Check your accuracy.

7. If you missed even one name, try using the preceding four-step memory process again. Remember, these are valuable customers, who will be offended if they are called by the wrong name!

If you are working alone, ask someone to compose a customer name list so you can practice using this communication tool.

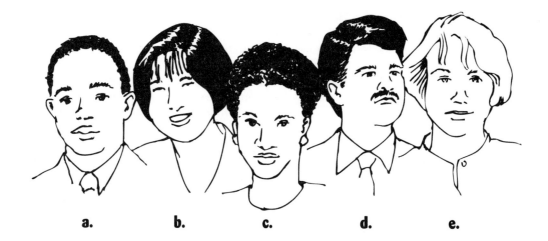

Customer a.

_____

_____

_____

Customer b.

_____

_____

_____

Customer c.

_____

_____

_____

Customer d.

_____

_____

_____

Customer e.

_____

_____

_____

"The ability to remember names is not an inherited gift. It is just plain work plus the desire to 'want to'!"—Dale Carnegie

Customers: What Else Do They Want?

Customers have more basic needs than just to feel good because someone knows their names. According to Abraham Maslow, these basic human needs are:

1. **Air, water, food, physical well-being:** If customers come in while you are very busy, offer them a cup of coffee or tea so they will be more comfortable while waiting for you.

WORLD OF WORK   Several businesses offer complimentary cups of different beverages for customers who are waiting. A large eye clinic also has water, cookies, and candy available for its patients. Some places provide children's toys, crayons, and books for waiting clients and their children. In each of these examples, the employers make an organized effort to meet some basic needs of the external customer—the need for water, food, or physical comfort.

---

2. **Safety:** The next basic need is the need to be safe. If customers want to "help" in the shop, it will be essential to stress the need for them to stay in safe areas, perhaps by painting "Don't Go Beyond This Line" on the shop floor. If this does not work, a partitioned waiting area with chairs, magazines, and newspapers can be developed to keep them safe.
3. **Financial security:** Financial security is the next basic need. This need is especially important to consider in giving cost estimates to customers or clients. When you think the costs will exceed your original estimate, *be sure* to explain this information promptly. To retain your customers, *do not* let extra costs come as a surprise when the customers receive the bill! A surprise price increase will probably be the quickest way to cause them to feel financially insecure and go elsewhere with their business.
4. **Friendship:** Another basic human need is the desire for friendship. It is important for you to maintain a level of friendship with your customers. This does not mean inviting them home for dinner, but it does mean treating them as individuals and not as strangers who happened to walk in off the street. This can be accomplished by remembering such things as their preferences in color, style, football teams, or food. Being able to talk with others about their particular choices is a way to deal with them as valued individuals rather than as just another number in the files.
5. **Succeeding on the job and in life:** Succeeding on the job is the final basic need. When others tell you about their employment promotions and successes, remember to congratulate them. This recognition can serve as one more communication tool to utilize to maintain effective customer relations. It will be equally important to congratulate your co-workers on their achievements because you will be acknowledging their worth and value to the company (adapted from material quoted in Lamberton and Minor, 89).

After thinking about these five basic human needs, you can see why it is difficult to talk to someone about financial security if that person is hungry, has no place to live, or feels the surroundings are unsafe. The first three needs usually must be fulfilled in the order of their priority before a person is truly able to focus on numbers four and five.

The basic needs of human beings must be considered if one is to relate successfully to different types of customers. Sometimes customers may focus on one specific need and not progress through them in this orderly five-step process. Be prepared to accommodate this difference. For some people, financial security is much more important than feeling safe. These individuals will need detailed cost estimates, *not* "around $100.00." Otherwise, they may feel cheated or taken advantage of and will take their business elsewhere.

In addition to knowing the importance of basic human needs, understanding *perceptual* differences will be a great advantage when communicating with customers and co-workers.

6.2 PERCEPTION

What is perception and how does the perceptual process affect communicating with others?

Webster's New World Dictionary (1986) defines the process of perception as "the mental grasp and interpretation of people, situations and objects by means of the five senses" (p. 1054).

Being able to understand a situation from the customer's point of view is vital for successful communication.

WORLD OF WORK   Often, when dealing with customers and co-workers, there are differences in the perception of a situation. Customers may think you are ignoring them because you do not speak to them right away. They may think you no longer care about their needs when you are just trying to finish a job that was due an hour ago. In that same situation, a co-worker may be annoyed that you are not helping on her or his project as you had promised.

Because you cannot perceive 100 percent of everything you observe, touch, taste, smell, or hear, misunderstandings often occur. This gap in perception between what we think we know and what is actually happening can produce a river of misunderstanding between ourselves and others.

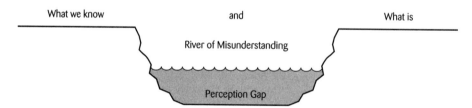

Selection is the first part of a three-step process for bridging this "river." Usually, we select the things that are the most obvious to us and focus on what is most familiar.

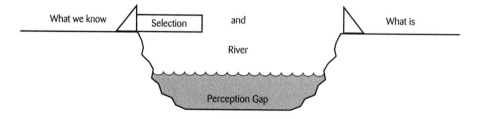

If a customer brings a car that isn't running right to an automobile technician, the technician will probably "hear" motor sounds an untrained ear will never detect. The technician selects those sounds because they are familiar noises.

Organization is the second step in bridging the river of perceptual misunderstanding.

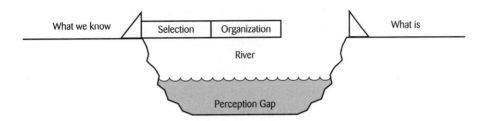

The most common ways for organizing this information that has been selected are:

1. **Grouping** often causes people and things to be placed in stereotyped categories. For example, a customer with red hair becomes angry and someone assumes that *all* redheads have bad tempers.

2. **Figure/ground** relates to the judgment that one part of a person or an object is more important than the other and everything else recedes into the background. *Another* redheaded customer comes into the area, and the focus is on that red hair. Consequently, it is expected that he will start yelling, too, just because he has red hair.

> Here's a visual example of figure/ground organization.
>
> *What do you see here?*
>
> *This geometrical figure could represent a partially filled glass, a refrigerator, or a window that's almost closed. Each person decides where to focus and what will be the foreground/figure, then what will be the background.*

3. **Closure.** This mental process demonstrates the need for the completion of a task or a relationship. Suppose a regular weekly customer suddenly quits coming in to do business, and no one knows why. It can be productive to contact that customer in order to find out why, rather than guess about the reason for the absence. The cause could be illness, dissatisfaction with the work, or a move out of town. The origin can perhaps be determined and corrected if there is a way to resolve the problem for the lost customer.

   Showing interest in the customer could motivate him or her to continue to do business. A personal contact brings the situation to closure and is much better than assuming the customer is angry.

The final step in the bridge-building process is labeled **interpretation.** Interpretation is based on a person's cultural values, beliefs, expectations, past experiences, and norms of behavior. Customers from other countries often will have very different perceptions of the proper way to conduct business. They may expect to engage in some friendly conversation prior to doing business because it is important to get to know a person before you can trust this person to be involved in any business transaction. But what if you are from the United States, have an appointment in five minutes, are very time conscious, and just want to find out what the customer from overseas wants so you can get to your appointment on time. The customer's interpretation may be that you are unfriendly and rude, and that he cannot complete this undertaking with a stranger who takes so little time to become acquainted with customers. Your interpretation is that this person is wasting time because he will not get to the point about what he really wants, but keeps asking about your family. Misinterpreting the situation may cause each of you to lose money since you did not try to understand each other's point of view.

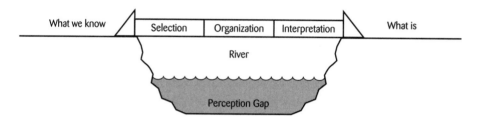

TOOLBOX OF THE TRADE

Instructions

With a partner, brainstorm at least five ideas about how you could handle the preceding problem of relating to a customer whose cultural expectation is that friendships are more important than being on time for the next appointment. Share your ideas with the class.

If you are working alone, how many ideas can you think of for solving this problem caused by a cultural misunderstanding?

Since no person can possibly select, organize, and interpret everything at the same time and because of individual and cultural differences, it is necessary to use another communication tool, the tool of **perception checking.**

A perception check is useful when dealing with others in order to determine the correct interpretation of their behavior. Using this technique reduces defensiveness in others because it enables you to check the accuracy of your assumptions.

The perception check tool is implemented by following this four-step process:

1. Step 1: Describe the behavior (action) that was observed.
2. Step 2: Give one possible nonjudgmental reason (interpretation) for the behavior that was observed.
3. Step 3: Give another *very* different possible reason for what happened. This one should also be nonjudgmental.
4. Step 4: Ask for a response.

It will be necessary to use a calm, pleasant tone of voice and direct eye contact while employing this tool. Negativity and sarcasm will hinder effective communication.

Example:

1. *Step 1*
   Alice says: "When you walked out of the office and slammed the door." [Behavior description]
2. *Step 2*
   Alice says: "Were you in a hurry?" [interpretation 1]

   OR
3. *Step 3*
   Alice says: "Were you mad?" [interpretation 2]
4. *Step 4*
   Alice says: "Was there another reason you slammed the door?" [asking for a response]

TOOLS OF COMMUNICATION

Instructions
Practice using the four-step perception check tool. Compare your answers with a partner. This communication tool can also be used by a team working together to develop the responses.

Exercise 1

After you give the customer his order, he looks at you and frowns

1. Describe the behavior you observed and say to the customer:

_____

_____

_____

2. Interpretation 1:

_____

_____

_____

3. Interpretation 2:

_____

_____

_____

4. Ask for a response:

_____

_____

_____

Exercise 2

When the customer is asked how she likes the repair work that was just finished, the customer says, "Well, it's O.K."

Supervisor says:

1. Describing behavior:

_____

_____

_____

2. Interpretation 1:

_____

_____

_____

3. Interpretation 2:

_____

_____

_____

4. Ask for a response:

_____

_____

_____

In addition to the direct questions and paraphrasing discussed and practiced in Chapter Four, the perception check can be a useful communication tool for relating to customers on the telephone as well as in person.

6.3 CUSTOMERS ON THE TELEPHONE

Talking to customers on the telephone and answering business calls courteously are essential to job success. There are effective ways to answer and make business calls.

When communicating with customers on the phone, what are the specific points to remember in order to be more effective?

Identify yourself and the firm at once in a cheerful voice, for example "Jones and Company, Joe Smith speaking." When answering for others, avoid abruptness. Don't say, "Who's calling?" It's more polite to ask, "May I tell her who's calling, please?" or "How may I help you?"

Give courteous attention to callers' requests and/or complaints. Let the callers tell their own version of what happened in their own way instead of hurrying them or trying to tell them what they want.

In getting additional information, be tactful, avoid asking needless questions, and use the customer's name whenever possible. For example "Joe, I'm sorry the part didn't get here when we promised. Will next week work for you?"

Always remember to keep your promise if you agree to call back. A broken promise can mean an angry customer.

Record the complete information neatly, including the time and date of the call. Be sure to paraphrase for accuracy.

When it is necessary to leave the phone, give the caller a choice of waiting or having a return call. Customers will appreciate concern for their time. If the callers are placed on hold, return every thirty to sixty seconds to ask them if they want to continue to hold. Another response to this development could be:

> *Thank you for calling us. We really want to serve you, but right now we are very busy. Will you please call back in twenty minutes so we will be able to help you more efficiently?*
>
> *or*
>
> *Thank you for calling, we are very busy right now. Please leave your number and we will return your call within the next hour.*

Express appreciation for all calls, and close them courteously.

When communicating with difficult customers on the phone:

- If the person is angry, make notes and tell the caller you are doing this.
- When you make notes, callers know you are interested enough to write down their complaints.
- Also, summarize and paraphrase what the person has said. This will tell the caller you do understand his or her position, needs, and frustrations.
- When calling someone who will talk too long if allowed, start the conversation with: "Good morning Mary, I have three questions for you."
- If a call seems as if it won't end, inject "Just one more thing before we hang up . . ."

When initiating a call to another company as a representative of your own company:

- **Identify yourself** and your company's name quickly. Next, give the name of the contact person in the company.
- **State the reason for calling** briefly and directly.
- **Before placing telephone orders,** write out all specifications to avoid confusion or delay.
- **If the purpose of the call is to make a complaint,** explain the problem calmly and courteously. You will receive better attention by avoiding accusations, irritation, and impatience.
- **Conclude all business calls pleasantly** and promptly by thanking the contact person. (*Association and Society Manager*)

Customers and the Telephone

Instructions

Working with three others, plan a realistic telephone response to an angry customer who calls to complain about a job that is late. Take turns answering the customer and calling as the customer. The third person audio tapes the responses and plays them back. Evaluate one another's answers.

- Which responses are the most effective?

- Which responses are the least effective?

- What could be done to improve the telephone techniques?

6.4 RESPONDING TO CRITICAL CUSTOMERS

WORLD OF WORK   Good service has always been the main reason for customers to do return business. One supervisor said the cost of finding a new customer is five times greater than the cost of keeping a present customer happy. However, the unhappy customer will tell eight to ten people about a bad experience with a company.

So what can you do if an angry or critical customer telephones or comes to talk to you in person?

Customers need to know the business cares about their needs. This can be accomplished by giving them your undivided attention.

In the beginning, just listen to angry customers. Let them vent. Do not interrupt or try to explain. Then:

1. Get more details by
   a. Getting specific information through:
      (1) Paraphrasing
      (2) Asking direct questions such as:
         (a) What do you want me to do on this project?
         (b) When did you expect the job to be done?
   b. You may even need to guess about what is wrong—for example: "Is it our service you are unhappy with?"
   c. Ask what the customer wants—for example: "Do you want us to redo the work or refund your money?"
   d. Ask if anything else is wrong—for example: "Are there any other problems with the repairs we made?"
2. Agree with customer.
   a. Acknowledge the truth of what they say—for example: "I understand you expected this job would be finished this week."
   b. Their opinion—for example: "I realize you thought your job would cost less than this amount."

3. Suggest a solution—for example: "May we loan you a substitute until yours is ready?"
4. End on a positive note. You may not always win over all the customers to your opinion, but at least thank them for bringing the problem to your attention.

All of these responses will probably not be used at the same time or with *every* angry customer. Use only those responses most appropriate to the current situation.

"Love your enemies, for they tell you your faults."–Benjamin Franklin

---

How to Relate to Critical Customers

Instructions
Work with a partner to develop responses to the following criticism. Share your solutions with the class. The class can discuss and vote on the two best problem-solving teams. If you are working alone, discuss the situation with a friend and ask him or her to work with you on this project.

Customer: "You told me this job would be reasonable, and now you say it will cost $294.00. No way is that price reasonable. I thought this was an honest shop! What's more, that's not the color you told me it would be. You said it would be brown, but this color is almost black."

1. *First,* **listen** and **don't interrupt** or explain.

2. Then get more details about the specific information by:

    a. Paraphrasing

    b. Asking direct questions

    c. Guessing what is wrong

    d. Asking what the customer wants

    e. Asking if anything else is wrong

3. Agree with the customer:

    a. The truth of what they say

    b. Their opinion

4. Suggest a solution

5. End on a positive note

Remember, *all* of these responses will not be given to *every* customer; however, some of them can be very helpful when dealing with irate customers.

　　171

6.5 UNDERSTANDING CULTURAL DIFFERENCES

When dealing with customers from other cultures it is very important to be aware of cultural differences. Cultural variations in business procedures can occur in organizations, in different parts of the city, in various geographic regions of this nation as well as globally. Some cultural differences appear when:

- Two different age groups start to communicate, and differing value systems emerge. One may desire quality products and the other prefer quantity production.
- One person is more interested in direct communication while conducting business, but the other person wants to establish a relationship prior to getting down to the details of a business transition.
- Someone wants to talk in generalities about the issues involved in creating designs, planning work, vacation schedules, and the like, and the second person wants to elaborate on the specific details.
- An employer, employee, or customer insists on jumping ahead of the chain of command rather than trying to solve a problem at the immediate level. Some will view this "I want to see the boss" attitude as a power play.
- Personal and family needs are given higher priorities than commitment to the work or the company.
- A new employee is expected to know how to accomplish a task but is given no directions about *how* to do it.

WORLD OF WORK   An American employee who was working in Argentina quit a job that paid well because he could not adjust to the Argentine style of socializing with business prospects before *any* decisions about orders were made. His preference was to do business and leave the country instead of waiting to get to know the people prior to business transactions.

When a person communicates across cultures, sometimes it is necessary to begin business discussions with seemingly trivial topics to establish some personal relationship before others are ready to talk about the work that needs to be done. Such a conversation could start with questions like these:

"How was your flight?"

"How's your family?"

"What's the weather like at this time of year where you come from?"

"What do you like to do in your free time?"

Understanding and valuing differences is essential to the success of both customer sales and service. Success is more likely to occur if you take time to research the values of other cultures when relating to people from other parts of the world or even in different areas of the United States.

If workers do not learn to adjust to personal and cultural differences, then issues of harassment may arise.

What is harassment? Is it something that occurs once, or is it a behavior that is repeated? **Harassment** was defined by multicultural specialist Denise Osei as "Any type of behavior that causes an employee or customer to feel uncomfortable. This could be classified as repeated offending behavior or a significant one-time attack, either verbal or nonverbal." Harassment by co-workers and/or leaders is often the cause of costly lawsuits, large cash settlements to victims, and/or the dismissal of the offender. *Any* type of harassment creates a negative work environment. Note the real-life situations reported in the case studies included in this chapter. Unfortunately, these examples are typical of work situations where people have differing value systems.

STRESS LESS Before going home, allow yourself time to relax in order to deal with what is happening on the home front in a relaxed manner. To accomplish this, try the following relaxation technique. Sit in your car or on a bench in a waiting area, close your eyes, and breathe deeply for five minutes.

CASE STUDY 1 *Joe continually complains that you are slacking off and not producing as much work as the rest of the team. Joe also says your work is not of good quality and your coffee breaks are too long. These comments are made repeatedly in front of everyone in the break room.*

Work with a partner to decide how you would handle this situation if you were the person being harassed.

Then discuss how a supervisor should handle the next problem.

CASE STUDY 2 *You are the supervisor, and observe the following situation as it develops.*

*A customer with an accent walks up to buy some supplies and your employee at the counter keeps asking the customer to repeat what he wants. Finally, the customer gets what he needs and starts to leave. The employee turns to a co-worker and says in a rather loud voice, "If **these people** are going to live here, why don't they learn to speak English so you can understand them."*

How would you handle the immediate situation with the customer?

How would you follow up this situation with the employee(s)?

CHAPTER PROJECT: ORAL REPORTS **Instructions**

Use the format on page 175 to prepare an outline for a sales, service, or technical presentation. Make sure it includes at least two of the five basic human needs listed previously in this chapter. Work as a team of three to five members Select the type of presentation you will prepare. The choice will be either listeners with no knowledge of your career or listeners who are experts from your field. Give a

15- to 20-minute group presentation to the class. If possible, videotape the class presentation for more accurate self-evaluation. Feedback from other students and the instructor is very useful in assessing the presentation strengths and weaknesses.

The following format is a guideline for this report:

Oral Presentation

I. The general purpose of the oral report is:
   A. To give—within a time frame—the facts, figures, and information necessary to the listeners to understand the subject you are presenting.
   B. To present the information in an interesting style.
II. The specific purpose of this assignment is:
   A. To give you an opportunity to present the same subject matter for two different types of listeners. (Choose 1 or 2.)
      1. The oral report will be given for listeners who have no knowledge of this field. The listeners may include business people, students, or politicians.
      2. The audience is a group of experts from your particular field or specialists from your general area of business or industry.
   B. To know as much as possible about the audience so you can adjust your presentation to their knowledge.
III. Make your presentation interesting and energetic.
   A. Both untrained and trained people are human beings; they react favorably to talks that are vital and dynamic.
      1. The material needs to be so well organized and so carefully thought out that it will have real value .
      2. The presentation needs to be effective, conversational and detailed.
      3. It is necessary to communicate with energy and enthusiasm, and to use direct eye contact when speaking to the listeners.
   B. The introduction and the conclusion are very important to a presentation prepared for either type of audience.
   C. Use visual aids because they usually will add to the understanding of the information.
   D. Use verbal supports to help the audience understand each major idea that is presented, because ideas must be carefully supported with proof. These would include:
      1. Definitions
      2. Facts
      3. Statistics
      4. Examples
      5. Quotations
         a) From experts
         b) From customers
      6. Comparisons with other products
IV. Prepare an outline for the report. Designate who is responsible for which part of the presentation.
   A. The outline for each speech must include the following to be complete:

1. Title of the speech
2. Introduction
3. Body
4. Conclusion
5. Works cited (listing any information from outside sources)
   a) Printed information
   b) Individuals interviewed
      (1) Name, position, and company
      (2) Place, city, and state
      (3) Date and time

   B. Give the outline to the instructor at the time of the presentation.

V. Use note cards to speak. Statistics and quotations need to be visualized to have a greater impact. If visual aids (flip chart, posters, etc.) are utilized, be sure the print is large enough to be seen by every person in the room.

VI. To make this presentation as professional as possible, a person may feel more prepared by wearing business-type clothing.

   A. For a man, it is appropriate to wear a shirt, a tie, and a sweater or sports jacket.

   B. For a woman, it is acceptable to choose a simple dress, a suit, or nice slacks and a jacket.

   C. For a shop presentation, it is all right to wear clothing suitable for the situation.

VII. Feel mentally excited about sharing your ideas, and the presentation will be outstanding.

What Does an Outline Look Like?

Title

Introduction

Create interest	I.	
		A.
		B.
Specific purpose (thesis statement)	II.	

What are the main ideas you will discuss?

Body

First main idea	I.	
Supporting details		A.
		B.
Second main idea	II.	
		A.
		B.

Conclusion

Summarize	I.
Action or challenge	II.

The organization of ideas will help you to remember the main points to include. When talking with any group, use two to five main ideas with supporting details, including logical and emotional support. A well-thought-out organization makes it much easier for listeners to enjoy hearing your ideas.

Oral Presentation Evaluation Form

Class members and the instructor can use this evaluation form to provide feedback for the oral presentation team members.

Speaker: _____   Evaluator's name: _____

Title: _____   Date: _____

	Poor	Fair	Good	Excellent
CONTENT:				
Introduction:				
Gained attention.				
Made purpose clear.				
Body of speech:				
Well organized				
Interesting ideas with supporting details				
Emotional supports				
Logical supports				
Conclusion:				
Summary				
Created lasting impression.				
DELIVERY:				
Confidence, enthusiasm				
Voice:				
Loud enough				
Interesting				
Body action:				
Posture				
Gestures				
Eye contact:				
Overall impression of speech:				

COMMENTS:

DISCUSSION QUESTIONS

1. Do you agree with the concept that co-workers should be classified as internal customers? Why or why not?
2. Do you believe co-workers should be given greater consideration by the employer than external customers? Why or why not?
3. Would your ranking of basic human needs be the same as Maslow's as listed on page 163. If not, where would you differ?
4. What are some cultural differences you have noticed between individuals?

SUMMARY

In this chapter, you had the opportunity to use some communication tools essential to communicating successfully with customers and co-workers. These tools were:

-   Learning names quickly
-   Using the telephone effectively
-   Checking perception accurately
-   Responding to criticism productively
-   Understanding and relating to cultural differences
-   Practicing an oral team presentation

If you believe you are proficient in using these communication tools, then you are ready to move to the next chapter, working in teams. If you cannot apply them automatically, now would be a good time to review this chapter and practice using the skills until you feel confident.

CHAPTER SEVEN

Teamwork: Communicating Productively with Co-workers

LEARNING OBJECTIVES

1. Discover other trends in the workplace of the future.
2. Learn about creating positive communication climates with co-workers.
3. Learn about and practice communicating nondefensively.
4. Learn and practice giving and receiving instructions productively.
5. Analyze leadership styles.
6. Learn to give orders effectively.
7. Learn to solve problems creatively.

Industrial relations managers, personnel directors, and supervisors from every type of business and industry in all parts of the United States have declared that communication tools are important—often critical—to success *on* the job. Many of these forward-looking employers refer to their employees as *internal* customers because they are as valuable to the company as the more traditional *external* customer.

When you think about yourself working for the company of your choice—a plant, a shop, a hospital, or a computer center—what do you think about? Are you visualizing yourself utilizing the skills you are learning in your field, such as building new equipment or using the latest technology to maintain it?

Undoubtedly, you are seeing yourself successful with the abilities necessary for advancing on the job. But do you see yourself with more than just the essential skills? Do you see yourself communicating effectively with other employees? A successful employee is the man or woman who works well with others and communicates effectively, not only with external customers, but also with co-workers, the internal customers. This chapter will focus on the tools needed to communicate productively as a team member or team leader in the workplace of the future.

7.1 WHAT ARE OTHER TRENDS IN THE FUTURE?

What will be the nature of the workplace of the future?

The vice-president of marketing and public relations at Washington Water Power, Joanne Mathison, recently discussed this future workplace and the skills and abilities employees will need to be successful. She stated that the forces of change are:

- Increasing competition
- Advancing technology
- Environmental issues
- Additional customer demands

This workplace will probably have just one supervisor for fifty people, with fewer management positions. In addition, employee and supervisor roles are changing.

Ms. Mathison stressed the changing employment contract. These differences in the work agreement can be described as:

- Management that is changing from a paternalistic attitude ("We'll take care of you") to empowering employees with the attitude "We'll help you take care of yourselves"
- Employees who will create job security for themselves through learning to become more "employable" by developing the ability to perform a variety of skills in order to be part of work teams, no matter what the future brings
- Disappearance of clear career paths because employers need workers who can learn to adapt to rapidly changing technology, often for short periods of time
- Employment relationships that are ceasing to be long term, with more temporary employees contracted outside of the company, and these "temps" are working for many different companies in a lifetime

Because of these changes, self-managed work teams are developing. Employees are taking on more responsibility and more of the traditional supervisor's role. In addition, employees will work to resolve their own conflicts. Another important aspect of these self-managed teams will be the need for employees to be multi-skilled and able to function in various roles.

Future employees will work together to become problem solvers and trainers as well as learners. Self-managed groups have different team structures. These vary in the length of time they work together to accomplish a goal or complete a task, as well as the amount of control and authority the team possesses.

Short-term task force teams usually have a single focus, such as improving work schedules or planning a design for a special project. Groups with longer time commitments often work together in preparing quality products for customers, when the team is responsible for the entire process from the beginning to the end (Mathison Lecture).

WORLD OF WORK   A local trailer manufacturing company assigns its employees to teams. Each team is entirely responsible for the production, quality, and the time spent in the completion of one specific type of trailer.

Most employers desire the following teamwork skills in their employees:

- Efficient listening
- Effective feedback
- Productive communication with external customers and co-workers
- Explicit instructions, both in giving and receiving them
- Creative problem solving
- The ability to issue orders and requests nondefensively

WORLD OF WORK   During a 1996 team-building seminar, the director of materials for Sacred Heart Medical Center, Bruce Currer, presented convincing evidence of the effectiveness of work teams. He stated that in the last year their printing services department had been able to increase output by 20 percent and reduce jobs printed late by 40 percent. This was accomplished with no additional staffing through the implementation of work teams.

Because of information from employers and data from the previous employer surveys, this chapter will concentrate on discovering how to communicate in order to utilize one another's strengths and differences more efficiently. One of the most helpful analyses of information has to do with the awareness and understanding of individual styles of communication, presented in Chapter One. This understanding can aid in building positive communication climates in the workplace.

7.2 BUILDING A POSITIVE COMMUNICATION CLIMATE

Realizing that it is often difficult to achieve *efficient* communication, and knowing the many benefits of good communication, you will want to develop some specific communication skills that can be valuable to the ongoing maintenance of work teams. To develop strong job relationships by communicating in teams, start with the following techniques:

1. Choose the correct time and place for sharing ideas with your team. Rush hour is *not* a good time to discuss a creative solution to a problem or a change in work schedules.
2. Speak with a definite goal in mind. Do not just start to talk hoping that something significant will come out of your mouth.

    a. Think before speaking. This is necessary in order to deliver the message you want others to receive.

    b. Plan what you will say, whether you are asking for a raise or want someone to trade shifts with you.

3. Respect the dignity of others when you are speaking.

    a. Speak with honesty, but be aware of the feelings, needs, and interests of others.

    b. Remember, it is constructive to question an idea, but it is destructive to attack a human being. (See Section 7.4 for five communication techniques to present ideas in a constructive manner.)

    c. If the suggestions your leader makes concerning production changes are unacceptable, discuss them privately with the leader. Don't say, "That was a stupid idea." Instead, focus on the work. Then ask a question, like, "What did you want to accomplish with the changes in production?"

4. Realize that others respond verbally in the same manner they are approached. If someone speaks to you angrily, your natural inclination will be to reply with anger. It takes maturity to change negative communication to positive communication. You can do this by avoiding sarcasm, expressions of boredom, or any other form of negative communication that puts others on the defensive.

5. Listen objectively. Realize that you, too, have prejudices and attitudes that can keep you from having an open mind about what is being said.

    a. Understand that you may interpret a message incorrectly. People often hear only what they expect to hear, not what is actually said.

    b. Practice using the paraphrasing tool discussed in Chapter Four and perception checking in Chapter Six.

6. Avoid withdrawing or becoming alienated from others. These reactions only close the doors to understanding.

7. Understand that we all are different because of our many experiences in life. When you respect differences and communicate with them in mind, others will appreciate your understanding. Remember that those with alternative methods for accomplishing tasks are not deficient workers simply because their methods are different from yours.

8. Strive to build trust. Trust comes when there is acceptance of others. This does not mean that you will always agree with others, but it does allow honesty and openness.

9. Verify the degrees of your continued success while communicating.

    a. Ask questions, and observe the listener's response, both verbal and nonverbal.

    b. Paraphrase a statement such as, "I'll be finished soon," by responding with, "Do you mean five minutes or thirty minutes?"

    c. Search for feedback.

Because every human being has the right to courteous communication, it is essential to treat co-workers with the same respect that you would give external customers.

Respecting co-workers, the "internal customers," also involves the communication tools discussed in Chapter Six:

1. Learn their names, by using some of the name-remembering techniques.
2. Recognize that co-workers, the *internal* customers, have the same basic human needs as the *external* customers.
3. Strive to understand those with cultural differences.

When these techniques for building a positive communication climate are used, it will probably be easier to maintain a productive work environment. A negative workplace environment lowers employee morale and reduces productivity.

What are some factors that create positive or negative work environments?

Work Climate

Communication Tools for a Productive Workplace	Factors That Contribute to Unproductive Working Conditions
Words like "please" and "thank you" are used to show respect for others.	Commands such as "Come here immediately!" or "Repair this now!" are used constantly.
Criticism or correction is given privately.	Criticism of other workers is given in front of the rest of the team.
Disagreements with the supervisor are discussed privately with that person.	Workers make fun of a supervisor when he/she is not present.
Schedules are discussed with the appropriate person rather than complaining to those who have no control over them.	Workers complain or whine about work schedules and vacation times continually and have a "That's not fair!" attitude.

WORLD OF WORK "Everybody likes to be noticed. But too often we toil in obscurity," asserts L. M. Sixel in the *Houston Chronicle*. He goes on to point out: "Bosses just don't give enough compliments. Some don't ever say a nice word about a nice job; others may give an occasional pat on the back, but it rings hollow. Praise may sound like a fuzzy feel-good topic — smacking of a group hug in the middle of a meeting—but compliments are an important motivator at work. Done well, they stimulate more good work. But if they're done poorly—or not at all—it depresses morale." (D2).

7.3 NONDEFENSIVE COMMUNICATION

No matter how hard you try, sometimes positive communication climates just do not develop, and a negative, damaging, defensive climate takes over.

We use defensive communication when we feel under attack by another person so we put on a protective armor to avoid being hurt. Our "armor" is often composed of a counterattack on the critic, sarcasm, withdrawing, apathy or displacement (going home to yell at the dog).

If some different communication techniques are used, conflict often can be avoided or at least controlled to develop a nondefensive atmosphere between customers and/or team members.*

Technique #1

Describe the problem rather than evaluate it.
Say "This is late," **not** "You're too slow."
Instead of, "You are so disorganized, that's why we have to stay late," try "I get frustrated when we have to stay overtime and I have scheduled other things."

Technique #2

Work on trying to solve problems by being **problem-oriented** rather than trying to **control** all problems. When a conflict occurs within a team, be sure to get each member's opinion about the solution:
"This is what I want, so do it!" is not a problem-oriented statement. Instead, ask each person, preferably during a group meeting, but at least individually, "What can be done to solve this problem?" Then ask the group to evaluate and help to choose and implement the best ideas.

Technique #3

Develop empathy, feeling "with" the concerns of your team members rather than presenting an "I don't care" attitude.
For example, if someone says, "I'm late because my child is sick," and the team leader responds, "That's a personal problem, and I don't want to hear about it," this can make the employee feel devalued. Those who feel devalued usually do not develop strong company loyalty or energetic work habits.
Instead, when someone on the team tells you he or she is late because of a sick child, you might try paraphrasing: "It is frustrating to try to balance the needs of your family with the demands here at work." This reflects a caring attitude.

Technique #4

Avoid generalizations such as, "You are *always* late," or "You *never* do anything right." Instead, use an "I" statement: "I was frustrated when this job was late."

Technique #5

Treat others as equals to create an open atmosphere rather than putting yourself ahead of others. For example, instead of the team leader planning everyone's schedule and telling employees when, where, and how they will work, everyone might have input in planning the work schedule to create a positive climate.

---

*Adapted from Jack Gibbs, as quoted in Adler and Towne, pp. 379–384.

Nondefensive Communication

Instructions

Working in pairs, develop responses to the following situations using the previous five nondefensive communication techniques. After they are completed, share your solutions with the class and decide which are the most productive uses of these tools.

Situation 1: A long time employee comes to you and demands your immediate attention.

Technique
#1 Describe the problem, don't evaluate.

_____

#2 Ask employee to suggest solution.

_____

#3 Ask employee's feelings.

_____

#4 Express yourself by using "I" statements.

_____

#5 Treat the employee as an equal.

_____

Situation 2: A new employee wants you to explain how to accomplish some repair work and you are very busy.

Technique
#1 Describe the problem, don't evaluate.

_____

#2 Ask employee to suggest solution.

_____

#3 Ask employee's feelings.

_____

#4 Express yourself by using "I" statements.

_____

#5 Treat the employee as an equal.

_____

All five techniques will not be applied in every situation, but using at least one or two of these communication tools can reduce defensiveness in problem situations.

Using nondefensive communication techniques will also be helpful when giving and receiving instructions.

7.4 GIVING INSTRUCTIONS

We give and receive instructions almost daily about how to follow a procedure or to use a new product. In both our personal and our professional lives, instructions are frequently given and received in a haphazard manner, rather than being concise and organized. A team member or a team leader is often required to give and/or receive instructions, so knowing how to do this effectively will save time and money.

WORLD OF WORK   Bonneville Power in Washington state *requires* employees to know how to instruct other employees in the various methods the company uses.

The goal, when *giving* instructions, is **to have our meaning understood.**

When *receiving* instructions we often **assume** we understood what was meant, but as receivers, we need to **accept responsibility for understanding the instructions.**

If you practice giving and receiving instructions then you will improve your communication tools on the job, as well as personally! Be familiar with the material to be presented, and practice giving the instructions verbally.

When giving instructions, it is important to remember these points:

1. Get the attention of the instructee before beginning to give instructions. Establish rapport with your partner. Be friendly.
2. State the desired objective, the goal, or the overall picture.
3. Motivate instructees to want to carry out your directions by letting them know the benefits of following your directions. For instance, a person will be able to save time or money, or create a safer environment.
4. Know the instructee's technical vocabulary; relate to that person in terms of his or her experience. Obviously, you would not use technical computer terminology to give instructions to someone who is unfamiliar with a keyboard or an icon.
5. Give instructions in a logical sequence (time, space, topical): "First, do this. Then second, . . ." Use concise, clear language.
6. Establish a system of orientation: Use a clock face ("three o'clock," "six o'clock"); a map (north, south); up–down, right–left.
7. When giving instructions, give enough information to clarify but not to confuse. Information overload can cause some people to quit listening and create a breakdown in the communication circuit.
8. Use positive communication to overcome all possible language, physical, emotional and listening barriers.
9. Practice giving your instructions out loud. Use paraphrasing and ask for other types of feedback.
10. Remember to search for feedback after short units of information: check progress; establish a system of follow-up for the instructions.

During instructions on the job, follow-up is essential because you need to know that your instructions are being carried out. Go back to the person later to determine if your instructions are still being followed correctly.

Giving Instructions

1. Work in pairs.
2. Decide on a familiar task, tool, piece of equipment, instrument, game, or sport to use to give instructions to another person. Practice using visual aids so you can time yourself. Do not let your partner know what you will be doing ahead of time so you can make the instructions more realistic.
3. Plan the instructions to last a total of 7 to 9 minutes, including feedback from the person you are instructing. This means you probably will be able to deal with only some limited aspect of the total process.
4. Plan to set the scene for observers, including the place where instructions would be given and the person(s) involved. Plan what time of day you would be giving your instructions; time of day greatly influences the way it is necessary to communicate. (The last thirty minutes of the day are not an ideal time to give instructions!) It is always important to include the motivation for learning this process. Be enthusiastic—let the person know **why** the process is necessary, including the **when, where,** and **how** of the process.
5. Give your instructions in a logical, step-by-step order.
   a. Give each step slowly enough to be understood.
   b. Explain any technical terms. Think of what the instructee already knows and what else is needed for understanding.
   c. Use feedback to make certain the instructions are understood.
      (1) Do not ask, "Do you understand?" Instead, always phrase your questions so that you will know what is understood.
      (2) Ask the person to demonstrate how to follow your instructions in short steps and to tell you about each step using his or her own words.
6. Let the instructee return to the demonstration often. Use praise and appreciation when the instructee's actions are completed correctly and in a positive way. If correction is necessary, do it constructively.

The class can use the following evaluation forms to rate the effectiveness of both the instructor's directions and the instructee's responses. Divide the class in half. Assign half of the class to evaluate the instructor and the other half to provide feedback for the instructee. Midway through the class period, switch the evaluators' assignments.

Evaluator's Name _____

Giving Instructions Evaluation Form

Instructor: _____   Subject of Instructions: _____

Instructee: _____   Date: _____

How effectively did the instructor handle the following area of the instructions?

	POOR	FAIR	GOOD	EXCELLENT
1. Set the scene 　**a.** Place and time 　**b.** Individuals involved				
2. Gained attention of instructee before beginning				
3. Motivated instructee by giving the reasons for instruction				
4. Gave goal or overall picture of desired outcome				
5. Language used: 　**a.** Technical terms explained 　**b.** Clear, precise words used 　**c.** Avoided confusing details				
6. Logical step-by-step sequence 　**a.** Avoided backtracking 　**b.** Order of ideas was meaningful to instructee				
7. Used visual aids to demonstrate instructions being given				
8. Encouraged feedback from instructee: 　**a.** Asked for paraphrasing 　**b.** Welcomed questions 　**c.** Required feedback after short units of information 　**d.** Allowed for a return to demonstration				
9. Gave instructee encouragement and praise				
10. Sounded enthusiastic and interested: 　**a.** Could be easily heard 　**b.** Had variety in pitch and rate of speaking				

Evaluator _____

Instructee _____   Date _____

Instructor _____   Instructions _____

1. What kind of feedback did she or he provide the instructor? (Be specific)

2. How effectively was paraphrasing used? (Be specific, please.)

3. Did she or he ask to return the demonstration if the instructor did not ask for it?

4. Was there variety in the voice? Was enthusiasm communicated?

5. Other comments:

Understanding your preferred style of leadership is also a critical issue whether a person is working as a team member or in a position of leadership.

7.5 LEADERSHIP STYLES

When you are in situations of leadership, are you a "let's get the job done and get out of here" type of leader, or are you the type of leader who wants to discuss the problem as a group and get everyone to agree to a solution before making a decision?

Every team needs a leader who is able to maintain focus on the project, work, or task that needs to be accomplished. However, leaders who concentrate only on the job to be done may not be as efficient as they seem. They can miss valuable ideas and information because they do not consult all of the team members to evaluate and/or include their ideas.

Another reason for talking with other team members is that co-workers who contribute to the decision-making process will usually be more enthusiastic about the project when their ideas have been considered. Consultation causes team members to feel more valued as employees.

On the other hand, leaders who spend all their time talking about the task with team members and analyzing different approaches to the project can sometimes slow down production and miss important deadlines because they think one more bit of research or one more survey is needed. This type of leader may lose out because she or he suffers from the "paralysis of analysis" syndrome.

Copyright © 1999 by Allyn and Bacon.

WORLD OF WORK

An example of this second type of leadership occurred when a group of students were working together on a class project. Because they were so busy researching and analyzing the project, they failed to complete it on schedule and consequently received a low grade. Very similar analytical communication styles and people-oriented leadership styles afflicted this group with the "paralysis of analysis" syndrome.

If you are this type of leader, try to include some team members who will help you stay focused on the work that needs to be accomplished so your team can function more efficiently.

What is your personal style of leadership when working with a group?

All teams need leaders. It is useful to assess your preferred method for leading a group to determine your personal team fit. When you have completed the following leadership analysis, it would be helpful to ask two other people in the class, two close friends, or two co-workers if they have the same perception of you as a leader as you rated yourself. Color-code their responses on the leadership analysis form, and then write a thoughtful paragraph about your own perception of your leadership methods in comparison with others' perception of your style.

Leadership Analysis

The following factors explain different preferences in leadership. Rate each factor according to the way you think you would most likely react in each of these situations. Decide if you would act this way Usually, Often, Rarely, or Never. Then total the numbers at the end of each column. Consider *all* experience—work, school, church (any time you spent working with others).

	USUALLY 4	OFTEN 3	RARELY 2	NEVER 1
1. I usually act as the group leader and/or speaker.				
2. When leading a group, I would encourage working overtime.				
3. When leading a group, I prefer to let the team members create their own solutions to problems.				
4. When leading a group, I prefer to settle problems personally.				
5. Sometimes I am buried in details.				
6. I encourage competition between groups.				
7. I prefer keeping the work going rapidly.				
8. I believe the group leader should make the decisions about how, when, and what tasks need to be accomplished.				
9. I can easily express my ideas in a group.				
10. I believe team members should be encouraged to plan their own schedules.				
11. I believe it is the responsibility of the team leader to assign the work.				
12. I believe the team members should decide how fast work can be accomplished.				
13. I believe it is not necessary for group leaders to explain their decisions to team members.				
14. When leading the team, I would encourage the team to beat its previous record.				
15. I believe more work can be accomplished when team members follow standard procedures.				
TOTALS				

Now go back and circle numbers 1, 3, 5, 9, 10, 12, and 15. If your highest score is in the **Usually** and **Often** columns for these numbers, then you are a more people-oriented team leader. Now circle numbers 2, 4, 6, 7, 8, 11, 13, and 14. Add your score for these numbers in the **Usually** and **Often** columns. If these are higher, you are more task-oriented and would prefer focusing on the work that needs to be done rather than being concerned about the needs of the employees.

Copyright © 1999 by Allyn and Bacon.

What is the value of this analysis? When you have the opportunity to be part of a self-managed work team, remember this analysis of your leadership preference, so you can organize and/or be part of a team that uses the strengths of the various styles of communication and leadership. Most research has shown that productivity will increase and attitudes improve when employees are included in the decision-making process, because this creates a sense of worth and value in the employee.

No matter what the preferred style of leadership is analyzed to be, each team member is valued for his or her uniqueness and ability to contribute something of value to the team. The team leader who maintains a balance between completing tasks efficiently and relating to co-workers effectively will maintain the highest team morale.

WORLD OF WORK   During a committee meeting, the members were discussing the strengths and weaknesses of potential job applicants. Some members of the interview committee insisted on repeating the same information again and again. The meeting was in its third hour when one member said, "Look, I know I'm a task-oriented person and most of you are not, but I need to go home. We've been over this information several times, it's two hours past quitting time, so let's make a decision we can all live with and leave. " With that comment, they did return to the focus of the meeting, made a decision about hiring one of the applicants, and closed the meeting in fifteen minutes! This situation further reinforced the need to have at least *one* task-oriented person on a committee.

When a person is in team leadership, it is necessary to acquire some additional communication tools. Leaders need to know how to give orders effectively.

7.6 GIVING ORDERS

Your role as a team leader will be more challenging and satisfying if you learn the art of gaining the whole-hearted cooperation of everyone on the team. Often it may be your job to **issue orders** to others.

REMEMBER:

- Orders are given in order to *regulate the contributions of* various members of the team—to keep them from working in opposition to the purposes of the team and to accomplish the goals of the organization.
- Orders are *not* a power trip or a way to make you feel good.
- The guiding principle must be: Give only those orders that are necessary.
- People will be quick to judge the manner in which orders are given and may react negatively or defensively if orders are issued inappropriately.

It will be to your benefit to learn four different ways for giving orders to others. Even if you do not plan to be a team leader or supervisor, you may someday find yourself thrust into a leadership role. Learn effective methods for giving orders that will be helpful during your career advancement.

The four specific ways to give orders are:

1. **REQUEST.** The request form of an order is *most commonly used by good team leaders and supervisors,* and it will be wise to follow their example. You are probably already very familiar with several variations of the request.

   "As soon as you finish, Herb, will you please . . ."

   "Sally, how about giving me a hand with . . ."

   Most of what you set out to do may be accomplished by using the request method. It is a pleasant, easy way of asking other people to do something, but remember that a few people on the team, although they are excellent workers, must be treated carefully and not overused. The "request method" works particularly well with them. It does not irritate them. A direct command may remind these team members of the possible dictatorial methods of parents and teachers.

2. **SUGGESTION.** Often, an order can be disguised as a suggestion. *If you know your team members well, the hint will be more than sufficient*—for example:

   "We're supposed to get out ten units today, Mike, and we're a little behind. Do you think we can make it up before quitting time?"

   "Janet, are we doing everything we can to keep these records up to date?"

   This type of order, like the request, will usually start the ball rolling. If others are responsible and like to feel they have been consulted about the decisions, they will grasp the point of the suggestion immediately. In this situation, the members will usually take positive action to correct the situation. However, the *suggestion* is less effective with newer workers who do not have the background or experience to come up with sensible, practical solutions. Nor will the power of suggestion work with those who are undependable or incompetent. Often, the response is:

"I don't know."

"Maybe."

3. **CALL FOR VOLUNTEERS.** *Asking for voluntary assistance is a useful device in emergencies. Most people like the feeling of giving something extra to their jobs and often will want to help out in an unusual situation.* Use this distress signal with great restraint. One of the standard jokes among employees concerns the supervisor who regards each project as a "special rush." In all likelihood, the team member who will hear and respond to the call for volunteers most frequently is a friend; yet, even this loyal person will draw the line if the appeal is made too often!

4. **COMMAND.** *Sometimes, the command order is the only way to get something done, but use it as a last resort and then probably only in an emergency.* When this method is used, the team members will recognize it for what it is, because commands from parents and teachers have been a major experience in everyone's growing up process. Because working adults tend to feel they have left those commands behind, a direct command to one of your team members often is met with bitter antagonism. Such an emotional reaction is unfortunate, but the fact remains that the meaning of the command will be lost because emotions begin to take over. The only thing that will be clear to this person is that he or she is being ordered around.

As a team leader or supervisor, resign yourself to a simple fact:

At work, the direct command is to be avoided whenever possible. *And on those rare occasions when you must use it,* do so as calmly as possible.

Of course, the first thing to be sure of is that the most effective method of delivering orders has been chosen (request, suggestion, call for volunteers, or command). Then check to see if others have followed your orders to determine if the directions are clear.

If the job is not being done correctly, or if there is a feeling of irritation from those working with you, you can be reasonably sure your ability to issue orders needs improvement.

To make your orders clear:

- Speak at an understandable rate of speech.
- Watch your tone of voice.
- Assign work with a reasonable explanation of why, how, where, when, and what is supposed to happen.
- Check to see that each employee understands what she or he is told to do by asking for feedback.
- Be brief, direct, and to the point.
- Assign one job at a time whenever possible.
- Minimize your own importance.
- Use your authority frankly rather than in the name of top management.
- Work through the chain of command instead of sidestepping it.
- Be impartial in distributing tasks.

This list can be used as a periodic review. Ask yourself whether you are accomplishing each item on the list. When you can answer "yes" to each one, you will be able to give orders effectively. At any rate, the list will be a good measure of progress. As with any other skill, it takes practice to become proficient at giving orders successfully. Complete the following exercise to test your skill in giving orders.

TOOLS OF COMMUNICATION

Giving Orders

Complete this assignment to develop expertise in the different styles of giving orders. Do this individually. When you have finished, work with four or five others and choose the most effective method and wording.

Your name: _____

Assume you are the team leader. In the space provided, identify the method to use in each situation (request, suggestion, call for volunteers, or command).

Also write the exact words to use when an order must be given.

1. A customer is on the telephone requesting some technical information about the Super-Clipper, a computer manufactured by your firm. On your team, Jim Clementi is best qualified to give the information. Ask him to take the phone call.

   Method used: _____

   Exact words used: _____

   _____

   _____

2. Your team is falling behind in its production schedule. The supervisor, Sandra, has specifically asked you to complete nine units today. You are the team leader, it is noon, and only three units have been finished. Give one type of order to speed things up.

   Method used: _____

   Exact words used: _____

   _____

   _____

3. You see smoke coming from a corner of the warehouse. Tell Bill to get a fire extinguisher and Sarah to phone 911.

   Method used: _____

   Exact words used: _____

   _____

   _____

4. You need the help of your assistant, Jane, to prepare a statistical report. She is working on a project of her own.

Method used: _____

Exact words used: _____

_____

_____

5. Henry Hanson's reports are especially messy and hard to read. Tell him to be neater in preparing his work.

Method used: _____

Exact words used: _____

_____

_____

6. Phil and May are concerned about doing anything that is not in their job description. Today there is an urgent need for help with some heavy work in the plant which will take about an hour. Ask them to report to that department in the plant.

Method used: _____

Exact words used: _____

_____

_____

7. The normal lunch hour schedule must be altered today because most of the team will be attending a special anniversary lunch. Unfortunately, one person on the team will have to stay at the office as troubleshooter until the lunch is over at about 2:00. Give someone this assignment.

Method used: _____

Exact words used: _____

_____

_____

8. Describe a situation involving the need to give orders in a difficult situation:

Method used: _____

Exact words used: _____

_____

_____

7.7 SYNERGY

What is **synergy**?
Is it a contagious disease?
No!
It's the energy formed by people who work in groups!

Depending on the group, this energy can be either negative or positive. Positive energy is generated when group members work together and increase each other's effectiveness. When group members fail to cooperate or display hostile attitudes, negative energy is produced.

WORLD OF WORK Effective small-group communication had a significant importance to 68 percent of the 180 employers surveyed in 1998.

Group Problem Solving

Working in groups to find solutions to problems or to manage conflict can create a positive, energy-producing environment. The six-step problem-solving method is an effective technique for generating positive energy.

The creative problem-solving sequence was developed as a discussion procedure for applying research findings about human creativity. It is based on the work of Alex Osborn, Sidney J. Parnes, and others associated with the Creative Problem Solving Institute. The pattern is most fittingly applied to problems for which there are many possible solutions, such as how to improve some product, alternative uses for idle buildings or tools, or any situation needing imaginative solutions.

This method can also be used when dealing with conflict in the workplace.

Problem-Solving Steps: The Creative Method

1. Analyze and define the problem by asking some of the following questions in your group:

    ⇒ What is the specific problem? What are the issues? Is money an issue? Use of time? Are there differences in facts, values, power, or ego?

    ⇒ Who is involved? Those in the shop, office or president of company?

    ⇒ How many are affected? The entire company or just a few teams?

    ⇒ What is the extent of the problem? Our department, the office, the city or state?

    ⇒ How long has it existed? Is it a new development, or an old one that has reemerged?

    ⇒ Any other pertinent questions.

2. Brainstorm *all* possible solutions and make no evaluations about the solutions. During this time, also forbid the use of killer responses like "We tried that once," "It costs too much," or "It won't work."

3. Decide on criteria for evaluating brainstormed solutions. Will the decision be based on cost? Creativity? Time? Evaluate each possible solution.

4. As a group, decide on the best solution. Make sure that everyone agrees, not just a majority. Those who are not in favor of an idea can often create roadblocks or may be unenthusiastic and cause delays.

5. Now decide how the group will put the solution into effect:

  ⇒ Who will be involved? Will everyone in this group be included, or will two or three people gather information and report back to the entire group?

  ⇒ How many should be informed? In person? With memos? All the company or just those in the department?

  ⇒ Are other groups involved?

  ⇒ What is the time period for planning—a week, a month, a year, or continuing?

  ⇒ What is the schedule for putting the solution into effect? When will you start and end the project, or is it indefinite?

6. Plan for follow-up.

  ⇒ Who will check the effectiveness of the solution?

  ⇒ The time frame? When will evaluation reports take place?

  ⇒ What should happen if the solution is not effective?

In order to understand how problems can be solved and decisions made through the use of the creative problem-solving sequence, it will be useful to practice this process.

TOOLS OF COMMUNICATION

Problem Solving—Part I

Divide the class into teams of four or five people. Each group will choose one of the following situations. Then, using the six-step problem-solving format, work to find a solution you would recommend to the team leader. Compare your solutions with those of other teams.

  If you are working alone, assume you are the team leader and must deal with one of the following situations. Follow the six-step format and write out your ideas for each step.

1. An employee is not performing a required routine procedure. As the supervisor, you ask about it. The person says the procedure is unnecessary and the job is going well without it. How would you motivate this employee?

2. You have developed a new system of work procedures that will provide substantial savings in both time and money. However, adopting the system will require your team to make major changes in their daily routines. What would be a good way to get their cooperation?

3. Your staff has completed an assignment exactly as you had asked that it be done. Now you discover that your instructions were wrong, and the job should have been done another way. How would you approach the members of your team in this situation?

4. A team member comes to you obviously very upset with a grievance against the company. After hearing the story, you realize that much of the problem is the employee's fault. As the team leader, how would you respond to this person?

continued

Problem-Solving Format—Part II

Choose one of the preceding situations and, as a team, develop solutions.

1. Analyze the problem. What are the issues?

_____

_____

2. Brainstorm all possible solutions. Remember, no idea is too wild.

_____

_____

3. Decide on the criteria of evaluation (e.g., time, money, creativity), and evaluate _each_ brainstormed idea.

_____

_____

4. As a team, choose the best solution.

_____

_____

5. Decide how you will implement your team's chosen solution (who will do what and when).

_____

_____

6. How and when will you know if your solution is working? What are the team's plans for follow-up?

_____

_____

In addition to these work situations, there are many other issues affecting communication with co-workers, customers, and employers. Continue to use this communication tool until your problem-solving skills become automatic.

WORLD OF WORK   "When I interview prospective employees, I am much more interested in their ability to work with others than their grade point average."—Supervisor, Hewlett-Packard Company, Spokane Division

STRESS LESS If you are the team leader, you may be causing stress unintentionally within your team by giving vague instructions, arranging rigid work schedules, or failing to recognize work that is accomplished ahead of schedule. When you are in a position of leadership, stress can be reduced by:

- Giving specific instructions
- Developing flexible work schedules that allow team members time to meet family commitments and deal with emergencies
- Giving praise and recognition for those who have exceeded work expectations

CASE STUDIES *A team leader has recently experienced the following situations with two different members of the team. Form classroom teams and, using the six-step problem-solving format, discuss how you would recommend that the leader handle these problems.*

Case 1

Joanna, a native of Brazil, tells you that Thomas keeps asking her to go out with him. He has done this at least three times a week since she started to work with his team six months ago. When she politely but firmly refuses him, he says things like, "I know all you women from South America are party animals and stay out all night, so how come you won't go out with me? I can show you a good time." She goes on to say that he has also recently been brushing against her every time he walks by her work station. What would you recommend?

Case 2

Joe has been working on your team for almost a year. During this time, Joe and Charlie have gotten to be good friends, so Joe thinks Charlie would not mind if he borrowed a splicer from his toolbox, since he left his at home and Charlie is not present to ask if he can borrow it. However, when Joe opens the toolbox he is very surprised to find some drugs—crack and some marijuana joints. Joe tells you, the team leader, about this situation. What are you going to do?

CHAPTER PROJECT ## Organizing a Company

This three-part project incorporates many of the communication tools presented in Chapter Seven as well as previous chapters. Perception checking, paraphrasing, using positive nonverbal communication, problem solving in teams, persuading others by appealing to their basic needs and desires, researching companies, and contacting local businesses on the phone or in person can all be developed as you work through Parts A, B and C of the final project. This project could also be of further assistance in building your network of employers.

Instructions

Part A: *Organizing Your Company*

Form teams with four or five members. Your team will be the members of your company. A notebook recording your progress and decisions will be turned in for a grade.

1. *Elect a team leader,* president of the company, or chair of the board. The title will be the choice of the group. Someone will also need to be responsible for recording plans. In addition you may need to set regular meeting dates outside of the allowed class time.
2. *Use the six-step problem-solving method* to brainstorm and decide on a product your company could produce or a service it could perform that would motivate others to invest in your company.
3. *Assign or volunteer for areas of responsibility.* These could include:
    a. *Analyze the market:* What do people want or need? How many people would buy the product or use the service?
    b. *Create advertisements:* Find out the cost of ads for radio, television, and newspapers. Be specific in designing ads. Samples are included at the end of this chapter.
    c. *Establish a location:* What is available? What is the cost? What other companies would be in competition? Create a map to mark the business property you plan to use. A local business realtor might help with this aspect.
    d. *Evaluate all expenses:* How much initial investment is needed for equipment, supplies, salaries, etc.? Contact other similar businesses, and explain the project. They usually are very cooperative in helping students to complete assignments of this nature. If some business person does give you an appointment, do not exceed the time set aside for you and be sure to send a thank you letter following such a meeting.

Part B: *Once your company has made its decisions on Part A of this project, prepare a 20- or 25-minute group sales presentation for the class* based on the sales outline in Chapter Six. Then:

1. *Decide how to motivate investors.* Appeal to their needs and desires to be safe, save money, and have fun when they use your product or service.
2. *Design sample ads for* the investors to see and/or hear.
3. *Visualize the costs for the investors:* Use charts, graphs, overhead transparencies, or handouts for the class investors to examine. It is usually ineffective to explain the expenses only verbally, because most people do not retain several numbers at a time when they are delivered *only* orally. If you choose to use a poster, make sure the figures are large enough to be seen by those at the back of the room, not just those in front. A well-organized computer presentation using a program such as Power Point can be very persuasive.
4. *If you want to sell a product,* try to have a sample available for investors to see, taste or smell.
5. *Designate who will present* which part.
6. *Practice, practice, practice* out loud. Time yourselves so that the group does not exceed the allotted period.
7. *Be sure to include attention-getting opening and closing comments* within the allowed time. There is nothing more boring than just *announcing* your product or service. Look at the difference between these two approaches:

"I want to show you our new food product"

vs.

"Are you usually tired when you go home from work and need to fix a meal? What will it be, pizza again? How about something inexpensive, nonfattening, time-saving, and

different? Our new food product, 'Super Suppers in a Bag,' can meet all of these needs for you!"
Which approach appeals to you as being more effective? You should close your sales presentation with similar thought-provoking ideas.

8. Also, allow three or four minutes for questions and answers from the investors (the class, in this situation) at the end of the group presentation. Someone from your group should also close the question and answer period by thanking the "investors" for their time and attention.

9. *Audiences in the business world and in the classroom* appreciate presentations that begin and end on time, so make every effort to stay within the time period.

10. *Use the feedback forms* on page 202 to evaluate one another's company presentations. The instructor will assign an evaluator for each person in the company and also will evaluate the presentations by the team leaders and team members.

Part C: *Investment Time!* This will take place after all groups have finished their presentations and company leaders have given a brief two- or three-minute review of their product or service. Part C is not graded or evaluated, but it does help you to determine the effectiveness of your group's presentation.

1. Each student has two $5,000 stock certificates printed at the end of this project (see page 203 for examples).

2. However, only one stock certificate can be invested in your *own* company.

3. You *must* diversify and choose another company for your second $5,000 investment. When you make this decision, you will need to say why you think this other company is a worthwhile investment as you give that company your $5,000 investment certificate.

4. The companies will then add up their investments, and the company with the most stock investors is the winner.

Criteria for Final Project Group Report

Graded on Parts A and B
A—Written
B—Oral
Part A will be evaluated by the instructor using the following criteria

1.	How effectively the group functions as a team	40 points
2.	Organization of the notebook	30 points
3.	Creativity	10 points
4.	Mechanics (spelling, sentence structure, punctuation)	20 points

Part B will be evaluated by the instructor using the following feedback forms. The instructor will award a maximum of 50 points for each participant.
Other class members will also provide feedback to the groups.
Part C will not be graded.

FEEDBACK FORM FOR GROUP LEADER

Leader's name: _____

Your name as observer: _____

As group leader during the group presentation

1. Does he or she keep the group on track?   YES   NO
   Comments:

2. Does he or she exert leadership when necessary?   YES   NO
   Comments:

3. Does he or she explain the group goal and achieve that goal?   YES   NO
   Comments:

4. Does he or she bring in nonactive members?   YES   NO
   Comments:

   Other comments: (regarding paraphrasing, eye contact, etc.)

GROUP FEEDBACK FORM FOR GROUP MEMBER

Name of person observed: _____

Your name as observer: _____

1. Does he or she seem active and interested in the group process during group presentation?
   (Circle and comment.)

| No Interest Observed | Some Interest Observed | Good Interest Observed | Excellent Interest Observed |

   Comments:

2. Does he or she keep up active nonverbal communication and eye contact with other group members?

| No Positive Nonverbal | Some Positive Nonverbal | Good Positive Nonverbal | Excellent Positive Nonverbal |

   Comments:

3. Does he or she *paraphrase* other group members to clarify what is said?

| No Paraphrasing | Some Paraphrasing | Good Paraphrasing | Excellent Paraphrasing |

   Comments:

(Salisbury, unpublished exercise)

Stock Certificate

$5,000.00

Name of Company or Product
invested in: _____

Name of Investor: _____

Sign here: _____

GUARANTEED & BONDED

Stock Certificate

$5,000.00

Name of Company or Product
invested in: _____

Name of Investor: _____

Sign here: _____

GUARANTEED & BONDED

DISCUSSION QUESTIONS

1. Are you aware of any additional trends or new developments in the work-place that pertain to your career? If so, describe them.
2. What are the communication factors that create a positive work climate for you? What factors contribute to a negative climate?
3. Do you agree with the analysis of your leadership style? Why or why not? What type of leadership appeals to you? What do you think happens when a person's score for the "task orientation" style of leadership is very close to the "people orientation" style?
4. When giving orders at work, which type of order do you respond to most quickly? Do you agree that the "command" type of order should be used as little as possible? Why or why not?

CHAPTER SUMMARY

This chapter gave you the opportunity to do the following:

- Learn about trends in the workplace.
- Learn about both positive and nondefensive communication.
- Give and understand productive instructions.
- Evaluate various leadership styles.
- Understand the process of giving effective orders.
- Work in creative problem-solving groups.

Understanding and using these processes will help you become more successful in your technical career.

References

Adler, Ronald B., & Towne, Neil. *Looking Out Looking In*. Fort Worth, TX: Harcourt Brace College Publishers, 1993.

Association and Society Manager. Los Angeles: Barrington Publications.

Boggs, Alison. "Engine Shop Greases Workers' Palms." *The Spokesman Review*, Vol. 14, December 1996, p. A1.

Bridges, William. *Jobshift: How to Prosper in a Workplace without Jobs*. Reading, MA: Addison-Wesley, 1994.

Clark, Val. "Employers' Survey Results," 1983, 1992, 1998.

Clark, Val (Director). *Moving into Your Future, Part I*. Video cassette, Cottage Video and Spokane Community College, 1995.

Currer, Bruce. Lecture, Spokane Community College, February 1996.

Employment Seminar. PBS/KSPS, Spokane, WA, February 11, 1996.

Guffey, Mary Ellen. *Business Communication News*, Spring 1995, p. 1.

Half, Robert. *USA Today*, July 18, 1989.

Jacobs, Joanne. "$ Off Track." *The Spokesman Review*, February 25, 1996, p. B5.

Jardine, Douglas. "The Pressure to Change." *Pacific Northwest Leadership Connections*, Spring–Summer 1996, p. B5.

Jones, Daniel. "Hearing Is Not Necessarily Listening." *Rekindle/ISFI*, March 1998, pp. 17, 18.

Kennedy, Joyce, & Morrow, Thomas. "Electronic Resume Revolution." Quoted in *Business Communication News*, Spring 1995, p. 2.

Lamberton, Lowell, & Minor, Leslie. *Human Relations: Strategies for Success*. Chicago: Irwin Mirror Press, 1995.

Le Boluf, Michael. *How to Win Customers and Keep Them for Life*.

Mathison, Joanne. "The Workplace of the Future." Conference presentation, 1995, Spokane, WA.

Nichols, R. A. "He Who Has Ears." Lecture audio tape, 1957.

Osai, Denise. *Moving into Your Future, Part I*. Video cassette, 1995.

Power of Listening, The. Film. CRM/McGraw-Hill, 1984.

Roach, Lois. "Skills Assessment," "Paraphrasing," and "Oral Reports." Unpublished exercises.

Rosenbluth, Hal F., & Peters, Diane McFerrin. *The Customer Comes Second*. New York: William Morrow, 1992.

Salisbury, Linda Seppa. "Creating a Company." Unpublished exercises, 1989.

Sixel, L. M. "Jobs Should Offer Praise and Raises." Quoted in *The Spokesman Review*, December 30, 1997, p. D2.

Smith, Ken. "Online: Just When You Thought Your Resume Was Complete." *Hosteur*, Fall 1995, p. 18.

"Sorry I Wasn't Listening." *Compressed Air Magazine*, June 1998, pp. 20–24.

Sperry Univac. Listening Seminar, *Participants' Workbook,* 1983.

"Stress." Cardiac Rehabilitation Center, Deaconess Medical Center, 1988, pp. 1–10.

U.S. Coordinating Council. *Job Finding Kit.*

Webster's New World Dictionary of the American Language, 2nd college ed. (Daniel B. Guraluik, editor-in-chief). New York: Simon & Schuster, 1986.

Index